# SING BY THE BURYING GROUND

# Sing by the Burying Ground

**ESSAYS**

**MARIANNE BORUCH**

Northwestern University Press
Evanston, Illinois

Northwestern University Press
www.nupress.northwestern.edu

Printed in the United States of America

10   9   8   7   6   5   4   3   2   1

ISBN 978-0-8101-4692-1 (paper)
ISBN 978-0-8101-4693-8 (ebook)

Cataloging-in-Publication data are available from the Library of Congress.

*dear Forrest*

*By measure. It was word and note . . .*

—Robert Frost

# CONTENTS

# PREFACE

For years I have understood the essay and the poem as kindred spirits, but usually my attempts at the former have been of a standard duration, twenty to thirty pages and, however odd, often written to be spoken first to a roomful of writers and dreamers.

Instead, most of the pieces in this book are what I called at first my "wee essays"—a beloved word in the UK and Australia, that *wee*, but confusing, I'm afraid, in the US. Thus the briefer ones have become in my mind "semi-essays," a term which of course brings its own puzzlement, going beyond the matter of size, their makeshift form triggered by surprise and ending a small number of pages later. Now I realize that *semi* suggests, too, an ongoing movement into something else, a next step, a becoming for good or ill. And that boy singing by the burying ground: I hear him singing, or trying to. Because he's worried, and in motion.

More clearly perhaps, each piece in this book pretty much follows American poet Wallace Stevens's defining take that "thought tends to collect in pools." Many of these pools contain pools that continue to strike me as largely accidental, thought becoming thought in spite of what I may have predicted or never wanted really. The fact that they are small and largely free of any preplanned shape is crucial to both their containment and their loose expanse, their independence from me and from any worldly insistence about what an essay should be. Though a few carry a clear intention toward half-light whatever wayward way, most have abandoned that workaday effort en route or shrugged it off from the start. There's the matter of closure too. Most of these end in an unanticipated silence—as poems often do—before spilling off to another pool, this time a mysterious thought-going-under. But where? Thus we are back to that *semi*, however briefly absorbed, to continue that walk past the burying ground. And holding one's breath is a part of that silence, that singing.

The threads that crisscross and encircle these essays take up the usual and the odd: poetry, of course, its use in a pandemic (and post-pandemic, if we ever truly make it there), but also the quietude of Trappist monks. And the list goes on: a puzzling knickknack in a thrift store; how poets fall into categories (solos, duos, flocks) as birds do. Pilgrimages to Michigan and to England to pay writerly homage; Woden, the ancient Scandinavian god of war *and* poetry; the Wright brothers' kooky idea to repurpose the bicycle into flight on a windswept lonely stretch of beach; a cadaver speaking in an anatomy lab; New Hampshire's "view tax" and how Auden's "Musée des Beaux Arts" should be levied for that too; women's hairstyles that stay put over decades; Saint Kevin and his blackbird à la Seamus Heaney. The fascinations of boredom, trouble, empathy, embarrassment, melodrama. The growing deafness of a friend and an acquaintance; my own, here too. And the remote edgy treasure of a Dorothy Wordsworth, a Sylvia Plath, a Laura Jensen, a Langston Hughes, a Ciaran Carson, and many others.

So often with these pieces, I saw that I needed to re-seek the company of writers to whom I've been drawn most of my life to figure *why*; to come at familiar, beloved work that newly worries me; to dig under roots; to (drone-like) take pictures through cracked windows of certain poems and the cultural-or-not surges and trends surrounding them. I wanted to upend the usual knee-jerk take on the canon / the almost canon / the used-to-be canon as a big yes or a big no and not merely move blithely on into what is, to me, still a new century. In this sense, my binoculars are aimed not back, not forward, but mostly in a wayward spiral up and down. The governing fact remains that these oddly eked-out pieces are uncertain experiments and honest attempts to understand what I consider the most mysterious and addictive literary genre we have.

About the book's title: I do see each essay under the shadow of Emily Dickinson's saving, unnerving remark in her April 26, 1862, letter to Thomas Wentworth Higginson, editor of the *Atlantic Monthly*, that her fate was to "sing, as the Boy does by the Burying Ground . . ." So it is for poets of any time or place. Certainly ours.

This preface, by the way, is not a wee essay, not even semi-essay—though I suppose in a certain light, it could be.

# SING BY THE BURYING GROUND

# THE TROUBLE GENE

Which must be in the body, and *felt* first. Because one clear thing about trouble—it can set you back to zero, a personal cone of silence. And reading, writing, listening allow entry into that troubled solitude; you disappear *into it* regardless of the time or place you really are, be it bed, kitchen, airport, elevated train, last week, two months ago, or two long weeks from now. We thin out and make room for what we read or write. That trouble orbits the oldest stone in us, back where quietude comes from. And poetry in there with it, our own trouble gene working overtime to pick up sound and shape.

What I mean is that not too long ago at a gathering of thirty or so where people loudly laughed and talked, a man I hadn't met seated next to me—mid-fifties, I guessed—seemed to cherish such a stone, even *be* one, eyes down, eating supper, no attempt at the usual chit-chat over the bedlam in that bad-acoustics room. I tried to talk to him. No luck. I tried again. Finally he looked my way, waved his hand—"too much ambient noise"—pointing to a device matchbox-small between his knife and spoon and my fork. I followed its wire to the small silver disc affixed to the side of his head. "My cochlear implant," he said.

A long-lost, beloved colleague of mine once used his deafness as a secret weapon for sanity and relief—turning his hearing aids off or at least down during departmental meetings that seemed to him point-less chatter. That was his favorite joke, a saving grace to a debilitating state that hits many of us as we age. Perhaps my dinner companion saw such a silver lining in that noisy room, this artist and graphic novelist from Detroit, Carl Wilson, his brilliant linocut prints documenting violent—and endearing—moments from his own life in the Black community.

But he and I were concerned that moment with hearing—his loss and my own—and a new way of dealing with that personal disaster. Shortly I would learn of the most unimaginable mic in the world, that cochlear implant as ear trumpet gone hip-digital and twenty-first century, talking straight to his brain via a magnet, how it had been slipped under his skin to link up that little gadget on the table to funnel in sound. That magnet business, as if words were steel shards, syllables as tiny lightning bolts pelting him. He realigned his wires, clipping the gizmo on the table to my shirt pocket. "I'm not being fresh," he said, "or maybe I am."

Thus began the etcetera of stranger to stranger, the well-meaning but awkward who-what-when-where of most conversation, right through dessert. Did that make our chat earthshaking? No. Just balance, pattern, the long-standing negotiation with the distance of another, that trouble gene sending out its auto-enzyme to refigure, resolve, or unresolve the world's complication in the sudden semi-quietude we briefly shared via our conversation in such a noisy room.

Semi-quietude. What I mean to say: on the brink of poetry.

I'm counting on analogy here.

———

It starts simple. Trouble and its noise, the great *out-there* again—vs. poetry. My *here* at a window, trying to think how this works. So many people live that audio wish to know through extraordinary methods, even down to a skull drilled to lay down a tiny metal plate inviting everything in. Poetry, too, registers inside and outside. Which may be why it's primal, endlessly valuable, repeatable, practically illegal, sleuth-like. Poetry: our need to hollow out a channel between self and world, self and self. Either way, you eavesdrop on who or what you don't quite know. A poem starts from scratch. Things weird-out from there thanks to the trouble gene, its range from one bird, one stone (or one bird, one decent pair of binoculars) to a mess of kaleidoscopic outback scrub, termite mounds, lonely and unsealed roads.

A stab at standard categories then: if the lyric is whisper, the *unlyric* (story or argument) is stage whisper, not secret at all but caught by readers and listeners who bend low to absorb what poets live, sometimes die quite literally, to say. The more classic lyric can take the drug straight to address a single individual, a beloved or the self, an I–thou or simply I–I. But there's a larger sense of audience, a communal responsibility in poems less lyric—an expansion. And it all means trouble.

It can go epic, that trouble gene working the ancient Sumerians into *Gilgamesh*, its authorship pinned to a someone or many someones as "He Who Sees the Deep," the story itself about a Trump-like ruler, though this one turns out well (or is a *Jane Austen*—my calling any happy ending). More instances: *Beowulf,* the Icelandic sagas, the intricate and weighty visions of Homer or Dante. Consider the Australian Indigenous Dreamtime stories of the oldest (seventy thousand years!) continuing culture on Earth. It's often a matter of desire and empathy turned mission, beyond the personal angst involved, more a matter of prophecy and history and moral weight spoken in the name of a collective intelligence, its rage or remorse or jubilation. A shared backstory and hope for the future at stake and, if part of the narrative at all, specific lives become singular examples, a line of breadcrumbs back into the primordial cave of being.

All because the trouble gene keeps bearing witness, riding tension, presenting the reigning horror show or whatever break in clouds lets in light. *I sing the body electric,* Whitman still shouts to high heaven, his me, me, me as *you*—no, it's *us,* underscoring poetry's *look-at-me* as *believe me, for god's sake!* An assumed citizenship out there, intent listeners. As with all art, trouble gets bigger before it resolves, if it does resolve. A journalist (however of the hack variety) before he discovered poetry, Whitman goes for curiosity and what's nonstop "breaking news." Think zoom lens and juxtaposition. And he won't shut up. But any poet must silence and trouble us enough to make us listen. Note this characteristic, eagle-eyed blurt from *Leaves of Grass,* 1855:

> The prostitute draggles her shawl, her bonnet bobs on her
>     tipsy and pimpled neck,
> The crowd laugh at her blackguard oaths, the men jeer
>     and wink to each other,
> (Miserable! I do not laugh at your oaths nor jeer you)

Similarly compelled, Langston Hughes in 1938 punched into his "Let America Be America Again" a parenthetical—"(America never was America to me)"—that stings like acid and sorrow gone flammable. A large poem, it's unnervingly relevant these eighty-plus years later, its fury and reach and inclusion regardless of phrasing at times as dated as Whitman's. Hughes's trouble gene is down every wretched road and passage.

> *Say, who are you that mumbles in the dark?*
> *And who are you that draws your veil across the stars?*

The poet's answer is a litany as specific as it is universal, including the speaker as "poor white," as "the Negro . . . the red man . . . the immigrant clutching . . . hope." It's a profound misery shared, that discovery of "the same old stupid plan / Of dog eat dog, of mighty crush the weak."

Of course, sweep and heft aren't always required. Dickinson, so often compact and abstract as she works the interior, throws her lot toward a chilling social critique too, one with a surprisingly worldly edge. Reconsider her #389, its rhetorical and narrative drive and invention, whose first line sets the scene and serves as a kind of title— "There's been a Death, in the Opposite House"—as this poet doubles down with unnerving detail of the house's "numb look," the traffic of neighbors coming and going, the doctor driving off, presumably having given up, until

> A Window opens like a Pod—
> Abrupt—mechanically—
>
> Somebody flings a Mattress out—
> The Children hurry by—
> They wonder if it died—on that—

Dickinson keeps taking on the town's heavyweights in this poem, ticking off the Minister who "owned all the Mourners" and the mortician—"the Man / Of the Appalling Trade"—who takes "the measure of the House—" And "There'll be that Dark Parade—" she wryly, chillingly writes, "Of Tassels—and of Coaches—soon. . . ."

The epic mode at any level is often launched by the agony of others. The passion to *do something*. There's the legendary true story of Anna Akhmatova taking to heart another woman's quiet plea outside Stalin's grim lock-up: *Can you describe this?* And she, urgently back—*I can*. And did, on tiny slips of paper memorized by friends before her words—destroy the evidence!—got thrown to fire, her poetry to be pieced together by what others recalled, for the future's unborn, for you and me.

The poems of Robert Frost's second book, *North of Boston*, came during an early self-exile in Britain though clearly he dragged New England with him for that short-lived but triumphant visit across the pond. "The Hill Wife," made of linked pieces, carries an epic impulse as in *beware, this could be your story, too*. Here the trouble gene can freeze a reader straight through.

### The Oft-Repeated Dream

She had no saying dark enough
For the dark pine that kept
Forever trying the window latch
Of the room where they slept.

And later:

And only one of the two
Was afraid in an oft-repeated dream
Of what the tree might do.

The poem's final section, its faint then fainter figure in the woods, must trouble anyone who lets it lodge in the brain more than five minutes. Its plainest of styles and the startling power of empathy play out in a way you'd never imagine empathetic: as reserve, as distance, a Frost feat and trademark. This habit of holding back appears simple but it's hard to pull off, his camerawork an opening pan, then a close-up before a more general sweep.

## The Impulse

It was too lonely for her there,
And too wild,
And since there were but two of them,
And no child,

And work was little in the house,
She was free,
And followed where he furrowed field,
Or felled tree.

She rested on a log and tossed
The fresh chips,
With a song only to herself
On her lips.

And once she went to break a bough
Of black alder.
She strayed so far she scarcely heard
When he called her—

And didn't answer—didn't speak—
Or return.
She stood, and then she ran and hid
In the fern.

He never found her, though he looked
Everywhere,
And he asked at her mother's house
Was she there.

Sudden and swift and light as that
The ties gave,
And he learned of finalities
Besides the grave.

Also from *North of Boston*, in Frost's most dream-soaked "After Apple-Picking," these offhand penultimate lines, loaded and so often quoted and loved—

> One can see what will trouble
> This sleep of mine, whatever sleep it is.

But "The Hill Wife" is an honest-to-god narrative that drifts toward epic proportions not only of loss but of the unshakable never-to-be-understood. He had that trouble gene down cold, by heart. It would not let go. I imagine this poem first came to Frost bravely solo as he remembered a secret left in those woods, a *should I*, a *could I*, a rare trepidation—blessed uncertain on-the-verge-of, and. . . .

Stop. Isn't that what poetry is? What it feels like as we enter its searing, mysterious company as readers or writers?

How to put this—

Every beginning is lyric.

———

Unlike in Frost's "The Hill Wife" where through gradual layering we learn how damage hits specifically then more generally, trouble can come as a jolt or a series of jolts, the silence huge before and after each hit. I recall but have lost track of where (and can't find either in a long ago talk he gave or an essay he wrote that has haunted me since) the rather panoramic way William Gass thought this might play out in fiction. You could be trudging across a snowy field and hear a stupendous crash, only to jerk around and see the long path you took—gone as a glacier calving abruptly into a slow blinding let-go. The route you'd been trusting: now only pure cold air behind you, down a mile straight. Nothing to do but stand there, dumbfounded, and count yourself utterly fortunate.

I admire poems that work like that. A dramatic recalculation to question what I was sure of, took no notice of, then. . . . One's dream life is at stake, one's fears, how brave one's been or hopes to be. Poem as *shape toward*—

Best is when you don't know toward *what*. Consider the sonnet, a poetic form we'll never get rid of because it really is the old *show your work* in math class, how the mind works through its most natural state: *worried*. The initial back and forth, to and fro—some call it *argument*—bears down to trigger a turn and change (volta, do your stuff!), and in that startle and pause you invert, reconsider, and *because of what went before*, it's *yikes!*, a revelation large or small. Something happens but *how* it happens to resolve or give up *is* the poem. The trouble gene insists on this. Most every other kind of poem is a ghost sonnet, following that drill however gone rogue, seemingly on its own steam—or in a sudden give-way, à la that William Gass analogy, every bit re-dreamt by a troubled descent down the page.

Here's one of the first poems I loved, a standout in an outdated anthology, a beautiful eerie piece written in 1930 at the height of the Depression by who-reads-him-now Archibald MacLeish, once a very big deal, the Library of Congress Poetry Consultant during World War II (the post renamed "Poet Laureate" for those coming after), a three-time Pulitzer winner (two for verse, one in drama), founder of UNESCO, on and on. (Note to every self out there: how truly unlasting the fairy dust of fame and fortune, if any comes at all. A few decent poems, if luck holds. . . .) Just reading MacLeish's spooky title back in my twenties, I was smitten straightaway and could not *not* read on.

### Epistle to Be Left in the Earth

. . . It is colder now,
        there are many stars,
            we are drifting
North by the Great Bear
        the leaves are falling,
The water is stone in the scooped rocks,
            to southward
Red sun grey air:
        the crows are
Slow on their crooked wings,
The jays have left us:
Long since we passed the flares of Orion.
Each man believes in his heart he will die.

Many have written last thoughts and last letters.
None know if our deaths are now or forever:
None know if this wandering earth will be found.

We lie down and snow covers our garments.
I pray you,
        you (if any open this writing)
Make in your mouths the words that were our names.
I will tell you all we have learned,
        I will tell you everything:
The earth is round,
        there are springs under the orchards,
The loam cuts with a blunt knife,
              beware of
Elms in thunder,
        the lights in the sky are stars—
We think they do not see,
        we think also
The trees do not know nor the leaves of the grasses hear us:
The birds too are ignorant.
              Do not listen.
Do not stand at dark in the open windows.
We before you have heard this:
              they are voices:
They are not words at all but the wind rising.
Also none among us has seen God.
(. . . We have thought often
The flaws of sun in the last and driving weather
Pointed to one tree but it was not so.)
As for the nights I warn you the nights are dangerous:
The wind changes at night and the dreams come.

It is very cold,
        there are strange stars near Arcturus,

Voices are crying an unknown name in the sky.

MacLeish's sobering jolts of trouble and silence get strange indeed and resist the culture-bound feel of much of his other work. Sentences here work as fragments do, suspended, the oddball white space shifting to suggest retrospect, a deep unknowing, a final piecemeal translation of ordinary days and years. The future looks back, the tone hypnotic, urgent then hopeless, the claims and imagery painfully contemporary. My guess is MacLeish himself was roundly taken aback by this piece that seems not so much a vision as a visitation. *Who wrote that?* he must have asked himself, coming out of his trance. How the world might remember it looked, the trouble gene in deep trouble, the poem's white space scattering logbook entries, simple advice, weather notes, astronomical readings.

Once more it's William Gass's deafening collapse behind us just when the world seemed stable, nondescript, an A-to-Z ho-hum. The trouble gene's roving enzyme keeps after serious trouble, looking for damage, change, discovery, reason through the white space of past and present, and now this *think again*. MacLeish's future tense warns us.

"Stanza" is the Italian word for "room," and poems made of such rooms can be as haunted as our *living rooms*, the very name replacing *front parlor* when undertakers took over what Dickinson called this "Appalling Trade" from households, out of the DIY mode to be fulltime modern Charons poling the dead over Lethe, River of Forgetfulness, setting up their funeral *parlors* as retail establishments on Main Street. Thus banished from the family home forever was any Great Aunt Bertha's "wake" or "viewing," complete with made-from-scratch funeral biscuits, those dark homemade party favors topped with a tiny sugar-iced hand rising out of a cloud. That room only for the *living* now, thus a major rethinking about communal space though that new name implies a previous haunting. And most *stanzas*, too, are ghosted by whatever trouble and silence hang there still.

For a number of weeks, I've been rewriting a poem based on *a thing that really happened*, hoping its parts add up. But the poem refuses to be. It hammers at me like tinnitus. Its details float about, trying to be some larger creature. A late-night darkness figures in, also my badly parked car when I discovered myself hemmed in. This, during a party, of sorts, and me early to leave, my car pinned in by other cars and my own damn fault.

Next to anything truly important—social justice, climate change, a sudden pandemic—my dilemma was a flyspeck, barely registering in the trouble zone. Still, there is a thing called "wiggle-room" in life and, perhaps, in art. It got literal, my *unjam, unjam thyself*—a mantra as I twisted and turned the wheel to reverse and drive out of there. Dark. Dark. Dark. I couldn't see much. Did I mention the fog?

Certain quiets get loud, however buried in the body next to weightier matters; those quiets keep welling up to bigger than they should be. One's called *panic*, the word cobbled off the mythic Pan whose pipes, in spite of their reputation for velvety seduction, were reportedly downright terrifying at times, used in warfare.

A young artist I hardly knew, Alexis Mitchell, left the gathering shortly after I did and was soon in that parking area, her *watchful*, her *wary*, arriving just in time. Who knew she'd turn spirit guide, rising up from the bleak nowhere next to my car to direct with her *keep going, veer right, now a little that way, okay, okay, now ease to the left*—practicing kindness on me as meticulously as a good musician does scales.

Gradually, somehow. . . . It just might work. I began thinking through that old film footage *slowly I turn, step by step, inch by inch, Niagara Falls!*, the Three Stooges shouting right out of their 1940s movie, the whole business rerun on television in the late '50s and early '60s when I saw it. As kids we repeatedly acted it out, screaming the phrase, dissolving in choked laughter. One loves things. For some reason or no reason. Now on a loop on a loop on a loop in my head, for a lifetime.

And my poor poem? Sentences don't necessarily complete what they start. They begin as glimpse, a bouquet's inch of bottom water right out of the tap clear as a lens, seemingly down there to juice up whatever cut roses. But there are other things quite beyond the power of our favorite never-to-be.

Hold up the vase. Idiot! Why did I drive into that parking place in the first place? Even Venus might lower her head, mumble into her clamshell embarrassed then mildly desperate: *Where are my clothes?*

Helping me inch out of the fix I was in, surely the young artist had her own reasons for generosity: that each day should end well enough for all, that she wasn't the only human in the world. Meanwhile, she was strong and smart. I was—okay—pathetic, going this way and that, just trying to make it out of there.

It got darker. To say *no moon* isn't to put the moon up there. But she had that trouble gene, an inkling.

# OH

Northfield, Minnesota. In the clutter of a thrift shop to raise money for good causes, I found a ceramic oddity of no foreseeable value. It made the opposite of noise—a silence in me, at once. Meaning everything flashing through my head stopped, abrupt, like how old elevators used to let go, then catch themselves in a half-second or two. You felt it. Various places—your bones, your belly. But you made it to the ground floor intact. Which is to say, you forgot quickly.

I haven't forgotten. It was—*is*, I still have it—a little white rocking chair to hold in the hand, simply and crudely made. *N.Y.C.* it says on the bottom but also *Japan*. There's a date, almost: a *19*, then two numbers smudged out. The rocker actually rocks. Black crosshatches on its arms and seat allude to, suggest, remind. . . . And that tiny crack barely visible on the back. Clearly, this chair has been loved and used. Had been. That's the key. On the high front of it, smack in the middle where a tiny head would lie back, are the famously plain initials: *J F K.* Oh, I thought, and sort of laughed because I figured tacky and poignant make a bad marriage, a terrible combo. In this age of irony, I'm a card-carrying member up there on a ledge, as ready as anyone to jump, looking down on the great sad expanse of the human story. But I narrowed, to a little *oh.*

At the counter a very old lady was tending to ancient matters of commerce. I set it down—oh, she said thoughtfully. A distant oh, a considerable way off. Then, oh. Again. That same silence pooled between us. How small the large can be, a pin, those angels who once danced there vanished. Being older, she must remember better than I can, I thought. His death, his life, surely a bigger dent in her.

Other people have looked—have locked—into it since. I have seen their faces churning up what was left of the past, their own or what was told to them. I said to a friend *close your eyes*, placing the little white rocker in her hand. Three seconds passed. When she opened—laughter.

Then, oh. Oh shit. Wow. After a bit: I was eight, she said.

That's more or less the range, from *ohshitwow* to the simpler, half-swallowed *oh*, but often a second and slower *oh*, as if cast underwater. Often that small hilarity, a sorrow-giggle, a ritual shake of the head. Enter the loaded shrug, as in: *isn't that just how it is?* Or, like the popular verbal punctuation, that two-syllable drop, the unanswerable suspended, its first note full of doubt pitched down, drawn out—*really?*—for nuance and critique. *Too much!* someone else said, rearing back on those two single stresses. Or *Get out of here!*—a phrase I hadn't heard in years, that seizure of teen disbelief.

The rocker is tacky. It's sturdy but slapdash-made. Worth a whole two dollars. I hesitated to buy it. Yet. *And yet*—that phrase, saddest in the English language, or so I've been told Henry James insisted. And the happiest? *Summer afternoon*, he said, like a secret is said, or like the most delicate and complicated insect burrows into a cool riverbank some hot July and the entomologists notice or dream they do, and tell you.

The little rocker triggers *funny* equals *sad* equals *strange*. How inward can you go until you hit poetry? Poems, too, are mostly small enough to fit the hand, and one line leads to another, each strata of attention another descent. And *oh* has been around, up from the 1530s, interjection of shock, bafflement, heartache, exhaustion, uncertainty, discovery—a common Indo-European word, out of Old French and Latin. Earlier that hour, before deciding my fate with it, I stood staring at that rocker among the once-loved, now-used-and-discarded objects on the thrift store shelves. You go empty, then drift toward something larger than anyone imagines alone.

It's as *over and over* as that, as immediate, the power of image. Is there poetry without poems? Wallace Stevens thought so. Still, poetry is a private act. And you do *write it down*. There's Gerard Manley Hopkins in his "Windhover"—"oh, air, pride, plume, here /

Buckle!"—or Whitman's "Oh me! Oh life! of the questions . . . recurring, / Of the endless trains of the faithless, of cities fill'd with the foolish," or Lucille Clifton's "oh antic God / return to me / my mother in her thirties." Or Anne Sexton: "I see the child in me writing, 'Oh.' / Oh, my dear, not why."

But that rocker, what it suggests and underscores, seems far from secret.

At the thrift shop counter, the woman looked long and deep at it, a witness. She'd been stopped back there, taking time to recover in public. Oh, she said again. The two dollars I held out to her seemed sacrilegious, a sudden and vast dumbing down.

———

Even a lapsed Catholic can love relics. But my little rocker wasn't of the "first-class" flesh-and-blood variety, certainly not like Saint Catherine's darkened clump of heart I once saw in Siena under a sign—*Absolutely no photographs!*—as a wave of Italians and Germans rushed through, madly clicking their cameras. No, and nothing like that wee chip of bone my brother said was probably from a chicken, passed off as a bit of the sanctified body, hot-pressed into thin plastic to protect and fancy up a holy card given to me in childhood. I've seen them for sale exactly thus, in a noisy piazza in Rome: *I swear, Miss, from Saint Anthony's ankle,* the man said, pointing to his own, *and only three Euros!* In grade school, my own radiant and gruesome stockpile of cards was held together by a thick rubber band, the many Blessed Mothers, a few Sacred Hearts tangled in thorns, my arsenal of saints including Agatha, her poor breasts severed and upright on a plate she carries like the most diligent waitress, walking forever in the color-spill of such cards. We girls collected them, traded them, most of us granddaughters of bent, babushkaed old women every morning in the pews before Mass slowly running the rosary through their fingers, bead by bead, my own Busia among them.

But my rocker wasn't a second-class relic either, not *something the saint touched*, the slain president definitely not a saint though there is that JFK holy card the nuns gave us not long after the assassination, as if he'd already been canonized. If there's a third variety of relic, maybe the rocker was it: a little thing to remind us, a most garish souvenir. Fake or real, such things can rivet. Years later, one laughs to rivet again, a double take. *Jesus.* Poignant, then tacky. Or the reverse. But there's that plaintive *oh* in there somewhere.

My husband points out such a rocker may not be a response to the shooting at all. Maybe kiln-fired earlier, *before*, a kind of hurrah, a token of tribute in 1960, a Welcome-Youngest-American-President-on-Record. I recall my mother at breakfast all those years ago, over the morning paper, the grainy AP post-election photographs: *And so good looking, too.* Still, I thought: this rocker *is* empty. That must mean something.

It was common knowledge—John F. Kennedy's notorious bad back. *Notorious* means *bad* to begin with, then into legend: that Harvard football injury, and the war-hero business, reverent facts raging through my parish thrilled by his election, pre-gossip, pre–Marilyn Monroe, et al. Therefore, his rocker—wicker, wood, homey, and just the right angle—that people said made him feel better day after day. He owned plenty, fourteen of them. "Whither I goest—it goes," he told reporters. Repeat, repeat. Keep rocking. Public, private, public, private until everyone gets the point and thus symbol, icon, cliché.

The rocking chair is a species, by nature redundant, defensive, a solace. It's a middling, low-key rain after an emphatic burst. You were rocked to sleep during such storms as a kid, if lucky. But some rain goes on and on, sideways crazy. Unlucky, dangerous hearts go a-fib, a-fib half the time, haywire, not redundant, not reliable. I like to think such a heart *fibs*, telling little lies to find its true ambition: think poetry, close and vast at the same time. Bring on the Trojan horse, everything kept real by imagining. Who knew there were thirty men crowded inside to change history, one particularly eccentric nun told us on a slow afternoon at St. Eugene's School. Thirty men, she said, men thinking they were an army. Is that a true fact, as my brother would say? All I could do was picture how it was inside that giant horse—airless, dark, not a word—the jerky stops and starts as it made its way through the gates of a shining doomed city.

The old lady puts my rocker in a small plastic sack logoed for another store: *Marty's Sweet Shop & More.* Clearly Marty's donation, a simple act of recycling—*repurposing*, I'm told now—was heroic, environmentally aware. But I wonder all the way back to the car what the "& More" might mean, what was involved even in the choice of a purple sack, a color remote and outrageous, found in the sea before clocks were invented, a substance in snails laid out in the sun to deepen over time to shades richer, taken by caravan or bandits to Venice and Toulouse, where the great dyers of the old world waited with their blue hands.

Later that week, I talk with a composer working hard on a piano trio, a first, a second movement winding down, a third in the offing. I show him the little rocker, and wait. I fear I'm starting to do this too much, getting a bit squirrely, like when artist Susan Woodson, my neighbor twenty years ago, said to me: Do you realize that *all* you talk about these days is birds?

That composer, Paul Brantley, keeps looking. Oh, he says. That familiar hit of laughter comes. He's a decade younger than I am. He was three years old when the assassination happened. Then he does what a composer does, by habit or genetics: he looks closer. Look! Holes! he says brightly, discovering three—two in the back, one in the bottom. And tries to play the thing. Presto, gets sound. He tells me—see? it's the beginning of *Für Elise*.

It is, it is. I hear Beethoven wringing his hands. I hear him making a go—more, a gift—of it. *For Elise*. I hear the beginning of greatness. It's a piece every piano student plays first, recitals jumpy and dull with it each spring. The rocker is upside-down as the composer seriously works out fingering on those two little holes and the larger one in the base.

Abruptly I think: my god, this is no keepsake or relic. It's a goddamn friggin' rockin' music-making JFK *saltshaker*. . . .

---

November, 1963. Middle of the country, north edge of Chicago. We were brief at it, the oldest kids St. Eugene's had, big-shot eighth graders just coming in from lunch, most of us having walked to our own houses for it, our mothers stay-at-homes, the standard drill for many women with children then. My mother with her canned peaches and cottage cheese, me with my peanut butter sandwich, we ate in front of the TV, turned on for her soaps, *The Guiding Light*, then *As the*

*World Turns*, old programs brought over from radio. But *it* happened later, at some moment in my walking back to school, against the jubilant shrieking I could hear on the playground a block away. Down in Texas, those shots, thousands of miles west and south.

Again: know-it-all eighth graders who might remember better, I suppose, or were old enough to understand. We got the school's only television, set high on some contraption rolled in on wheels, a cart the height of Father Barlow. It loomed over us, our fifty-plus gaggle of baby boom kids in one classroom. The nun walked forward and clicked the television on.

It opened to Walter Cronkite, whom I loved completely. What is private and what public? Is that confusion the beginning of poetry? In my memory, Cronkite calmly weeps as he talks, something close to *we don't know yet, can't confirm but we think*. . . . Tears slowly roll down his face, his words steady, somewhere between belief and disbelief, suspended in that nether-zone of hope.

*Children, this is what a very bad dream looks like*, our teacher said, a stricken Cassandra foreseeing everything, stock-still in her pre–Vatican II full habit, head to foot in black except for the starched white wimple that revealed a mysterious strand of reddish-blond hair. Human hair—impossible!

Walter Cronkite was impossible, crying. It was he who stunned. More than the shooting.

*Where were you when* . . . got asked for years. *Oh.* Everyone with a story—family, neighbors, friends repeatedly making their debut on the stage of history. (*I was at home, at work, walking the dog, I was in the grocery store, stopped cold, as the not-quite-right PA system at Jewel crackled out the news.* . . .) Poetry's *little* looks hard at *big*. How daring and moving the nerve of that, to assume a place in the grand scheme, stepping into a point of view as into a circle of light on the floor cast from a window suddenly blinding off the shady yard.

Here's a little rocker. Sit down; you must be tired, traveling such a long way.

Still, come on. A saltshaker? And someone really used it? Did it sit on a kitchen table for eggs, for the perfect mound of peas, for mashed potatoes? What about pepper—were there once two rockers, side by side, each adding its edge to a lifetime of breakfasts and suppers?

I found the answer the modern e-way, googling *shaker* and *JFK*. The chair was, in fact, for pepper. A frozen figurine of the man himself flashed on the computer screen, at ease in his rocker, his white shirt and tie. Kennedy full of . . . salt! Of course. Apparently a hole somewhere for its silvery flow. I looked back to my little rocker from where he'd been unseated. Then back to the computer—there he was, in miniature, relaxed in that chair again. *1962*, I read. Back once more to his banishment, my rocker empty. So goes erasure, a flipbook, quick, the endless-unto-nothing that poetry reveres and remembers. My husband was right; it was a tribute of sorts, before. But *after* is what happens.

I almost get it, how an everyday hand on automatic could reach at meals for both rocker and president, the mind behind such a gesture fully ho-hum about it, John Kennedy's rocker *repurposed*, enrolled in vocational school, given a real job. But the New Frontier, the Peace Corps, the Space Race all stamped *J F K* where a head should rest, on a tiny chair whose runners curve like crescent moons.

It's that salt thing. I love real stories. The ancient Salt Road is one of the great trade routes, back behind the Dark Ages, into the brain's mammal craving for salt, past that to its hard, gray reptilian root. Salt for all sides: so things *keep* and do not rot. Salt to enliven, to sharpen. Tears are salty. And blood. To *salt* the earth vicious and deadly in war means nothing grows, nothing of *home*, of *meadow* and *field* and *next day into next*, so the future stops *here* where all grief is communal, released, once private as a poem before it hits open air.

For salt, then. You'd have to hold the little figure at a slant toward whatever heaven, to shake and to shake. The minutiae of culture not even worth handing down except I am eye and ear to it now. And we have this taste in the world.

# PILGRIMAGE

If you drive north in the middle of the country above Indiana and toward Lake Superior, you'll find Saginaw halfway up on the so-called Michigan Mitt, at the webby slack point dipping down between thumb and forefinger, assuming the little-finger side faces west. If you enter that city, stop to fill up the gas tank, as I did, and ask about Roethke—born and raised there and early eager to get the hell out—the Mobil or Jiffy Gas guy might say to you what he said to me: You mean *Miss* Roethke? I had her in tenth-grade English. A hard-ass, for sure. But she knew her stuff.

So much for Theodore Roethke's only sibling, and thus it still rings true, his forlorn insistence that amounted to a more polite way of saying "no one in the state of Michigan gives a crap about me." But it's semi-untrue. There's a Roethke archives now in the town library, with the letters and papers his sister didn't censor or destroy out of black-sheep embarrassment, and the Friends of Theodore Roethke Foundation that keeps two houses sacred—built by the poet's father and uncle. In that Gratiot Avenue home where his sister June lived until her death a few years back, you can sit on the second floor "sleeping porch" as I did, and look out to where the Willliam Roethke Floral Company once stood—"twenty-five acres of roses under glass," as the poet liked to describe it—now a most unremarkable run of tract homes to be seen from those windows, weirdly placed, right in the heart of that city's great old houses. Another way to know the shape of his world, the boundary, the border between this replacement patch of now-suburban sprawl—"Roethke Court," it's been called—and the original rest of town, is this: you drive the circumference of that mid-twentieth-century development. You nose your car right to its edge, eying the ranch houses to one side, the street itself the divide; you *keep* driving, the sheer expanse—the breadth, the ambition—of *Wilhelm* Roethke's nursery quite astounding. His grandfather—morphed as was the immigrant's custom—to William.

On the upstairs porch though, you can *be* Theodore Roethke, maybe sick of the whole business, thirteen years old, hiding from the odious next chore of hauling topsoil or pinching back the upstart buds, a year away from the change in every bit of it, given his father's sudden death. You can squint and imagine the vast greenhouses out back, the manure machine rattling away all night kept ingeniously together with twist and wire, the roses and orchids, the tinted light of day in glass, the ancient nursery men, their smell of pipe tobacco, their muttering in German, the sweetness and anger, his mother's set time to bake for the week—that would be Wednesday. You can think, as in any pilgrimage: *here is where it starts.* The nerve, the vulnerability, the secret life triggered by boredom, dumb-dazzled up by the occasional high drama of years lived in that house. You'd be more than partly right.

Out there, where his "Child on Top of a Greenhouse" will have the speaker's feet "crackling splinters of glass and dried putty / The half-grown chrysanthemums staring up like accusers," where the old rose-house "rode it out," through the storm triumphant in his poem "Big Wind." You can wonder, as Robert Hass admitted outright in his essay that begins with a visit to Rilke's house in Vienna, how "actively stupid" it may well be to dog such a place, to sniff with such reverence, to assume somehow it *means.*

*I see by my outfit*, goes the famous spoof of the more famous Western folksong, *that I am a cowboy.* It is partly self-serving, maybe silly, this ritual, an age-old pressure to be present, of stepping-into.

A word from the red-eyed vireo on this: *Here I am*, the bird books translate—pause, pause—*where are you?* Languid ache, late afternoon, any woods you want.

One place few ever look for John Keats is on the Isle of Wight where it's life-threatening scary to rent a car and take to the narrow lanes. You keep sideswiping the bushes; you worry past—barely—every roadside stony wall. It's always the wrong side you drive. Bloody right it is. Your frantic starts and stops tell you that.

Keats loved that diamond-shaped island off of an island, one of the most southern parts of Britain—"a beautiful hilly country, with a glimpse of the sea," he wrote back about it—out of range completely from the chaos and filth of London. He was done with Guy's Hospital, with the medicine toward which he trained for several years, done with stricken bodies and illness itself—except his own, of course. His consumption. How could he *not* know by then, as a trained and tested surgeon-apothecary, very nearly a doctor in most people's eyes, caretaker to his brother Tom until death from tuberculosis freed them both six months earlier? On his second visit to the island, the poet holed up for a month, July into August, in the village which was, continues to be, Shanklin. An official plaque marks the spot:

> The rear part of these premises forms Egantine Cottage where John Keats stayed in 1819 writing "Otho the Great" and other works.

That "Otho" piece was purely for money, a play he agreed to co-write, the famed Shakespearian actor Edmund Kean ambitiously in mind though Keats already regretted it, felt himself "pretty much harnessed to . . . [that] dogcart" with Charles Brown, a friend who was visiting, eager to get the thing in order. "Other works" meant trying to finish two long poems, "Lamia" and "Hyperion," and to Fanny Brawne, his wannabe, nearly *intended*, letters so unbearably melodramatic that editors have held back some of them to save his reputation (or their own). Keats understood the risk, destroying the first letter—or so he claimed to Fanny herself in a subsequent exchange. Just too pathetic, at every point painful, though this passage made the editors' cut:

> I have two luxuries to brood over in my walks, your Loveliness and the hour of My death. O that I could have possession of them both in the same minute. I hate the world: it batters

too much the wings of my self-will, and would I could take a sweet poison from your lips to send me out of it. . . .

Be prepared. If you go to Shanklin—you can, you can even rent his room by day or week—it's unsettling to find on the "premises" where Keats wrote these words a magic shop called "Keats Cottage," whose sign reading "Gadgets Curios Gifts We Are Open" includes a familiar image of the poet. His chin rests on his hand, he's wearing the ruffled collar and cuff of the day, his dreamy look screwed up to see a future—just a guy his friend Brown sketched quickly on a dare, on a break from hacking out their tragedy, "Otho the Great."

Inside the shop, there's this alert: "Protected by witchcraft." Maybe a comforting thought, given the ghost involved. But no "first class" relics to revere, to look hushed upon, no going dazed in the looking. Which is to say, no evidence of Keats himself: certainly no shard of collarbone sealed in plastic as on a holy card, no lock of hair. No second-class relics either, nothing the saint touched—no glove or a bit of fabric from a shirt—unless you count walls and windows.

But everything is pilgrim-skewed and befits the place. On the shelves, intimate as suggestion, what doesn't grow Keatsian? Wry, then sad, then deadly earnest as his letters. It's all about transformation there, a netherworld of wonders, cheap stabs or ancient-strange. Charms and herbs and resins. Books on runes and dowsing rods, pentacles galore with metal strips to edge their bright glass, fairy-folk pamphlets of testimonials and sighting tips, lurid tattoos that last a week, witch puppets with broom or cauldron, you choose. A few corked-up blue-black bottles. Not eye of newt, but close. Do not drink.

Concerning poor, ongoing Otho and his greatness: "We are thinking of introducing an elephant," Keats wrote about the play to another friend in London that July, only half joking. Later, to Fanny Brawne: "I begin to dislike the very door-posts here."

———

Sometimes at home I walk down to the basement with some urgent reason to find or to fix. And getting there, *I have no idea*. I forgot! How long until my mother's advice comes back? Return to where you thought of whatever it was, that's all. And wait. I dumbly climb the stairs.

As if thought really is *in air*, I guess was her notion. Body, mind: never the source. Thought goes on quite without us, thank you. It's *outside* our *inside*. If we forget we only need quiet, patience, humility. Return to kitchen, bedroom, yard. Stand still. The *what* and *why* will re-descend. That's all it takes to remember.

But consider the pilgrim who acts on borrowed memory, where this great one got born or that cherished one breathed her last, who looked through this very window or never did. Who wrote this or wore that or said such and such here, or slept too much of the day, so at night . . . Where am I going with this?

Thought is portable. It's in the making: be empty, receptive, weird. Those troubling door-posts Keats wrote about, to Fanny? They refused to be forgotten. In act 4 of his *Otho*, they do worse than bother. They enrage and begin to stalk: "Do you forget that even the senseless door-posts / Are on the watch and gape . . . ?"

One has such hopes as a pilgrim. You'll catch a glimpse, a scent, a small and shared happy viral something. The very air—howbeit a million uncountable molecules—nearly two centuries' worth between then and now. *The Pilgrim's Progress* was a book my grand-father owned. I remember one engraving—the stiff-legged traveler with his little bag, startled by a seemingly uncrossable bog. It still fascinates, always some "slough of despond" to get over, to believe anything.

In the Shanklin magic shop, a few steps in the back to Keats's room, his door is made of tiny panes—the old, blurred, blown glass ridged, circles within circles that no one ever saw through. How vividly the world and its images outlast and matter-of-fact us.

―――――

Of many poignant, probably pointless memories, this floats through my head at the moment: in the cellar of Roethke's old Gratiot Avenue house in Saginaw, two or three ungainly trunks for serious journeys, long out of style, proudly stickered with exotic ovals, triangles, squares—maybe Paris, London, Dublin, Brussels. I can't remember. He traveled abroad one time, in the early 1960s, and to those places.

Upstairs, *poignant* has gone *endearing*: little index cards carefully typed with versions of his poems, set in the rooms they might best fit. "My Papa's Waltz"—"The whiskey on your breath / Could make a small boy dizzy"—pinned to the dining room wall. And "Dolor"—"I have known the inexorable sadness of pencils"—thumbtacked above a desk. More of them—how many?—all over the place.

Back in the cellar: *His steamer trunks*, I'm told, as if I need a caption. Relics then, honest-to-Zeus second-class relics: something the saint touched. Not precious, just distilled to simple use. You travel, you take your stuff. No melodrama, but it is *story*.

I'm nodding. I'm crossing my arms, thinking those trunks back into transit, in glad or even euphoric arrival, carried off the Norwegian ship that Roethke and his wife Beatrice took over the Atlantic or packed to the gills when they returned, the ordinary beloved detritus inside so crucial to the mystery of moving through a life. I imagine later someone shrugged: there is room for these trunks in the basement. Might need them; who knows? Down they went.

We might need poems, too, and stories, so Roethke's books wait on shelves, turned to now and then in passing, certain phrases committed to memory, to the body, with or without our knowing.

*I wake to sleep, and take my waking slow*, I read on a bulletin board last month at the university, and before I could blink—*and learn by going where I have to go*—I rattled off the rest of Roethke's poem, to my amazement.

We pass the time in a shared allegiance. It's not mourning, exactly. It's not praise, either. It *is* a curious pleasure—or just plain curious. We are strangers to those who leave themselves on paper, in words labored over or coming quickly once, with surprise—maybe worst and best—to unnerve them. It gets personal. It's bone deep. We can read them or *be* them, or something in the middle. *Influence*: writers are famously told to be anxious about it, to flee from it, to deny it. Guess what? It's there regardless, little knots and stray threads in the back of the tapestry called homage.

Hovercraft, the craft of hovering: *I know where you live* isn't always a threat. One can do this cornball writerly pilgrim thing. One can "make a visit," as we called it in my childhood, ducking into the empty church to sit and wonder whatever small thing. Go 3D, get the gist, soak it in. A real life makes the imaginary one possible. But it's real life we imagine in such places, before allegory, before Plath's blunt-brilliant poking with a stick.

You can forget why you came at all. For some, it's always practical. On the Isle of Wight, the man running the magic shop knew a good sales trick when he saw one. *Keats's Cottage*. What an outrage.

I like the Odes well enough, he said, just to the left of indifference.

———

The woman kindly showing me the cellar in the Roethke house kept pointing, neither bored nor boring in that catacomb, that cranny of a life left behind. She was devoted, a high school teacher in town, speaking slowly, each word treasured by silence first. I could barely hear what else she said. She loved what she was saying: *his* steamer trunks.

One whispers in a shrine, where a single pronoun can undo you.

# EMBARRASSMENT

⁓

has its uses. Here are two specific instances.

One: Dorothy Wordsworth, the famous William's sister, from whose extraordinary journal he stole some of the best bits for his poems. What she wrote there documents life at Dove Cottage, where they lived the lean, most fruitful years before he was fully invested among the English bards as a lofty hotshot. Word for word, those daffodils he lifted outright. And what else as they hiked miles together, she with that journal in hand or at hand, demonstrating her amazingly sharp eye without the usual village-explainer passages William would have added. She dived right into the thing itself, surrounded it with silence. On a day full of rain, "I made a shoe" she wrote. Or on a walk, meeting a boy of nine (who looked five) and alone, who "spoke gently & without complaint," she asked whether he "got enough to eat." Looking surprised, he said "nay." Then there were the roses no one planted that she noticed "in the hedges." I think of her as poetry's first imagist in English, before Ezra Pound and his irresistible grandstanding on the subject. Before West Coast poets like Gary Snyder humbled down to this word, that phrase to translate vast mountain/ sea/sky, believing the ancient Chinese haiku writers: *stunned* equals *only this much is humanly worth saying about that.* Before the image deepened for James Wright and Robert Bly via the usual Midwestern patience and stillness, beyond the latter's mind-altering rants. Dorothy Wordsworth had that sort of respect for the world-as-is, to *show* and not *tell.* I've heard only Coleridge noticed.

She was also toothless by forty. No pictures of her later life—
tintypes, paintings, drawings—have turned up. Did she ever openly
smile thereafter? I bet someone's written a dissertation on her "embarrassment issues." I see a connection. Her love of the succinct, what I
call the *beloved particular*—the image itself—seems the root of wonder, not the talk-talk overlay about it clogging up the passage from
world to self and out again. Embarrassment equals you step back, go
numb, and look hard at small things because all at once, you're small.
You guard, you monitor, you don't say much. But maybe you write.
(Cautionary tale from Miss Wordsworth: don't tell your brother.)

Two: My own mother in marching band, her French horn in hand.
How many times did she tell me this? Late thirties, small town, her
father in disgrace, and still. The uniform for girls: white skirt, navy
jacket. At some midpoint in the John Philip Sousa, she—here's the
usual veiled language—*got her period*, right there on the football
field, sweet October, the scent of burning leaves. A white skirt. That
colorful nightmare flood only women know how abrupt and *oh god*.
The girls broke rank, reshuffled themselves around her. And she in
her eighties, still so moved by their gesture, reliving it for me for the
hundredth time. Those old friends who shielded her, most of them
lost by then, the rest out of touch—she loved them.

This may well be mixing the sacred and the profane in the ser-
vice of some minor truth about embarrassment. Which is in fact
large. There's my poor mother in the mode of the body and its
foibles finding such loyalty and care. And that *other* Wordsworth,
same mode, she in shadow whom we should revere most, keeping her
mouth carefully shut but noticing everything, changing the course of
English-language poetry in the process. What both narratives share
falls under the laws of physics. But I'd reverse that classic dictum to
*what goes down must come up*. And consider the matter of scale—
however minute, next to the truly dire horrors of the world, the level
of dark in both stories at least meant: they knew now.

My mother liked to claim that we all get a peck of dirt to eat before
we die. After that marching band fiasco—open wide!—she probably gave herself three fat tablespoons to swallow, to shrink herself
down. Embarrassment first makes the self massive. But that self has a
way of reinventing, sized to normal by way of time passing, and this

chaser: gratitude for kindness and how the lasting sort can save and remake.

———

Which is to say embarrassment should be a matter of feeling godaw-ful in private until you get over it, though this danger is also possible: a standard and habitual self-savaging from then on. In any case, it could be a poem's most reliable fuel for propulsion in the nonstop flight halfway around a moment, an afternoon, a year, a life. That time you just couldn't *get it*—understanding nuance, what to do, what to say. The times of fear, if not trembling. The way some faces turn color but we all flash hot then cold. The terrible indecision of it, especially in the first half of a life, where everything still matters. The girl in it, the wee boy you were, the mythic staggering of self we keep close. The *where now* and *now what*. That smallness again, the huge *sudden* in orbit around it, adjectives turned instantly into nouns like that. The *quit-defining*. The *why-not-quit-everything*, the *about-to* hovering over the half-drunk water glass in hand, the *barely begun* bit of wine in a goblet. The prescription? Go inward. Go home, get quiet. Screw the party. Or just this conversation.

The loss of everything but the self has given us centuries of dis-turbing poems, that self as diminished, the world darkly looming up. Here's an extreme case, "I Am," by British poet John Clare, suppos-edly fully mad by 1845 when he wrote this piece in the Northampton General Lunatic Asylum, the last poem copied down by the house steward, one W. F. Knight. Here is what's handed us:

> I am: yet what I am none cares or knows,
> My friends forsake me like a memory lost;
> I am the self-consumer of my woes,
> They rise and vanish in oblivious host,
> Like shades in love and death's oblivion lost;
> And yet I am! and live with shadows tost
>
> Into the nothingness of scorn and noise,
> Into the living sea of waking dreams,
> Where there is neither sense of life nor joys,

But the vast shipwreck of my life's esteems;
And e'en the dearest—that I loved the best—
Are strange—nay, rather, stranger than the rest.

I long for scenes where man has never trod;
A place where woman never smil'd or wept;
There to abide with my creator, God,
And sleep as I in childhood sweetly slept:
Untroubling and untroubled where I lie;
The grass below—above the vaulted sky.

I sometimes like to "spot the cool bits" in old poems, radiant survivors that somehow aren't culture-bound, not filed away as "a product of their time." That's the real poetry in a poem. "And sleep as I in childhood sweetly slept: / Untroubling and untroubled"—the idea that even a short period in one's life could be seen as "untroubling" and not a source of worry, the poet freed, no longer second-guessing how others take stock—strikes me as an unscripted contemporary hiccup in the poem. There's joy in such longing. Or consider how his even ("e'en") those most loved "Are strange—nay, rather, stranger than the rest." That "rather" sounds sweetly offhand, so one-of-us as to suggest far more. Of course, I want to know *how* strange, what kind of *strange*, why *strange* gets the prize. That's where the garrulous poets of our era would flesh out gory details. John Clare is too embarrassed. That phrase—"into the nothingness of scorn and noise"—is pretty great too. It cuts to the quick, in line with Ezra Pound's emphatic *make it new* about whatever song or story some six decades later. What a brilliant way to reject rejection, to honor that universal impulse.

But note the source, the great dark of a mind which seems to have prompted this, the speaker/poet as "self-consumer of my woes." John Clare suffered greatly, must have spent years in the darkest of those darks. Still, the poet in him allowed him the solace of reordering pain, the grace of hearing words in his head not to heal exactly, but to acknowledge and steady. That "self-consumer of woes"—how near-officiously it catalogs despair, how unnerving and modern it sounds. Thus, *yes* to these moments that work on the brain to think past into present. Weirdly it's the reverse, too, how the present lives in the past.

Not because John Clare had lost his mind but because he had *not*, not completely. Not the crushing self-sorrow many of us are sane enough to understand.

———

Here's one last flash of embarrassment to prove the rule, though not nearly of the same order. Still, it was large and small at the same time: a younger cousin of mine at eight or nine, first day of the season at the local park's pool some long-ago June morning. Thrilled to be there, rushing the whole business in the changing room, slipping out of his T-shirt and shorts, speeding into sunlight, leaping into that perfectly contained, beautiful blue—to wave upon wave of laughter.

He had forgotten his swim trunks and, head down, climbing out, cupping his lower region as best he could, limped back to the locker room, mortified.

In my theory, this should have led him to poems. It did not.

# SPELLCHECK

⁓

Whose history I do not know. I do know I've been e-upbraided for my fast and loose spelling of the name of the ancient god Woden, whose last worshipper must have slipped under the sod during the medieval period, somewhere in the tenth century—imagine those bog-soaked, desperate sickbed prayers. (Just put out of mind the Alt-Right's current co-opting that archaic royal presence, his reputation narrowed, almost destroyed via their sick devotions.) And though that more recent deity, Spellcheck, made to keep the world on track, alerted me I was dead wrong on the laptop screen, this time it refused to save me. "No spelling suggestions," it archly stated, meaning: not even going to try. Machines can be so callow. They adolescent-shrug with the best of them. It happens that I have rather a crush on Woden, the only ancient god who, I'm told by a medievalist I trust—Dorsey Armstrong, who knows her time travel cold—arranged himself upside down for ten days to lure into his powers the gift of poetry, a nifty if unnerving shortcut for any poet. Here he was on my computer, no longer recognized by the e-know-it-all of the English language.

Thus I understood *Woden*, Anglo-Saxon god of poetry (yes, and war, then throw in learning and magic too) to be officially forgotten, his rich complexities e-pushed onto an ice floe. In one of his short prose pieces, "The Witness," Jorge Luis Borges laments the death of Woden's last worshipper as *example*, the end of a complicated mindset: a dug-in culture's bizarre take on a force, a shadow, a god, a raging mystery only half human. "What will die with me when I die?" Borges wrote to the future, disguised as his anonymous reader—though he is probably also talking to himself. What sort of "pitiful or perishable form will the world lose?" he adds. Fragile and vulnerable, details made stupid or brilliant by rage or love or *those awful times I did or didn't*. We leave behind; we take with us. Either could be the starting point—of what? Fear? Triumph? Poetry?

Bear with me.

You can always figure out the age of an older woman by her hairstyle, locked into place in her twenties; you do the math from there. Or so my grandmother, born in 1883, told me. She herself kept curling her hair with five-inch leather-covered wires which looked to me like overgrown, darkened string beans, no doubt bought in a shop with a little bell over the door in about 1906 and repaired by needle and thread over the years as the stitches frayed. She'd coil up her thin gray strands with them, set nightly in place with big black bobby pins. And never strayed from the look they engendered. I suppose that's been true for me, at twenty-two waylaid and stamped ever after, it seems, by the fashion of the day, my hair long and pulled back as so many other young women managed it in 1972, held fast with a simple elastic band. It was either that or a fab Twiggy-girl bowl cut, truly short, still a new thing then. But that required regular trips to the stylist to keep it short, which in turn demanded a consistent outlay of cash I didn't have. Besides, word was that you needed to be preternaturally skinny, nearly anorectic, to pull off such a look.

In so many other ways there's a *keeping on* in us past an expected expiration date, stubborn ghosts of habits vapid or profound, even dangerous, picked up to be doggedly—more like mindlessly—carried on. As poets, we absorb the quirks and biases and freedoms and limitations of our coming-of-age, and honor them pretty much forever. Irresistible, so communal at times, they're near lock-step. Thus, *history* set in stone beyond singular whim to define culture itself.

Maybe it's true that whole worldviews do just stop, kaput—à la Woden's last worshipper buried peacefully, if not burned or hung first. New thoughts take over, willed or by seeming accident. Consider those twentieth-century poets whose nerve we revere—Adrienne Rich, say, or Robert Lowell, James Wright, Allen Ginsberg, Gwendolyn Brooks—who started in more traditional ways of style and subject matter but at some point wildly boomeranged out and back to themselves, altered. Of course that's viral, too, the gestalt of the era. But as we age and keep writing, we leave behind what we can bear to lose by some river. Parting, whenever and however it happens: the weight, how suddenly light we feel is the poetry in it.

Thing leads to thing—yes, yes, yes, and bully for that. But both kinds of past (personal history, the world's history) have a lot to do with any future. I keep seeing the Wright brothers, Orville and Wilbur, nine Decembers in a row on a stretch of hard North Carolina sand near the sea, both from a land-locked expanse in Ohio, trying for *impossible*. To fly. Unlike Leonardo, whose drawings those brothers loved, no dreams of the moon for them—though, in ways similar to his, they studied wings, mostly birds airborne, against wind. And like Leonardo, they worked up images of unthinkable contraptions, erased, drew again, miming their hands just so to visualize fixed and movable bits in slow-motion wonder, how lamp sockets welcome the threaded base of a bulb. A flying *machine*. The flying part is ancient, is dream; the *machine* of it more recent and not genius but what might trigger it.

Because those brothers were, by trade, early aiders and abettors of that nineteenth-century craze: bicycles! Serious and diligent, they made them. Then, in their shop in Dayton, they sold them. That's the sweaty successful difference. Study the blueprints of *The Kitty-hawk*, named for the place in North Carolina—the aircraft's single, double-decker, crossbow-looking wing is delicate, huge, iconic now, jerry-rigged with modest chains and chain plates and hubs and crank arms right off their workbench, looking very much the standard parts of any bike, even the one the training wheels dropped from, your first shivering rush down the street as a kid, *lift off*, toward trees. And in their case, eventually to that vast nowhere of stars and planets and moons the brothers never really reached for. Recently I heard the following on NPR, quoted with no clear source, far beyond this subject: *They thought they had buried us, but they didn't know we were seeds.*

The believer whose eyes last closed on Woden may have been a brute or an angel or both—not unlike the rest of us—a hybrid though that god's specialty was fury. "Outside . . . a deep ditch clogged with dead leaves and an occasional wolf track in the black earth," Borges wrote, and "by now the sound of the bells is one of the habits of evening in the kingdoms of England. But this man, as a child, saw the face of Woden." And Borges imagines the details, what he claims the world forgot—"the holy dread and exultation, the rude wooden idol weighed down with Roman coins and heavy vestments, the sacrifice of horses, dogs, and prisoners."

And what happens if even just one of us dreams the old to make it new? (Ask yourself: Do you—or do those you read—write poems to be loved, or to discover? Either way, do you want a moral tale or a harder, stranger truth? Is it mending we're after, or to blow something up? To remember, or to forget?) As for those two obsessives from Ohio—a *flying* bicycle? Are you kidding? What an outrageous, dumb idea.

Wilbur haunts me, taken out relatively young, at forty-five, by typhoid. Wilbur who just a decade earlier stood in a doorway distracted, idly twisting an empty bicycle tube carton. Untwisting it. Twisting again, then: *Wing-warp!* (Would the great god Spellcheck distain and dismiss and counter that lovely phrase with its *wrong!*— "no spelling suggestions"?)

Slow it down. *Wing* plus *warp*, a *wing* that *warps*. A warping with wings. The lyric key, the seeming disconnect equals flight equals poetry. What perished when Wilbur Wright did? The feel of his hands on that small cardboard box. His fooling around changed gravity for us.

Because they shared every panic and pleasure, he looked up: *Where the hell is my brother?!* It was poetry, Wilbur's wanting to tell him.

# SAINT KEVIN, SAINT BLACKBIRD

Certain poems have inside them the source of all poems. I've thought this and probably said it many times. Because it is these I love instinctively, automatically—poems I read and reread. They share their bounty and radiate wildly, or so quietly. They return me—and, perhaps, others—to the reason one writes poems in the first place. This is not sentimental. This is fact, real as fable to haunt and light the way forward, back to prehistory. Which is only to say I've been stuck for a while, like the ever-present but archaic needle to whatever record (or to *vinyl*, as is said now) not on Seamus Heaney's well-known bog poems, admittedly quite wonderful, or on his childhood pieces dragging behind father and plow, but on his curious later poem "St Kevin and the Blackbird" which seems to me a brilliantly deadpan and plain *ars poetica* as much as—what's the word for *life* in Latin?—a *vita poetica*, if only our days could be seen so clearly. "And then there was St Kevin and the blackbird," the poet begins as though at the beginning of time. We are led carefully through the scene, the saint at prayer in his cell, one hand extended out the window where inexplicably, most wonderfully "a blackbird lands" and builds a nest. Inexplicably? Not really. When the eggs come, it is Kevin feeling their warmth over weeks and weeks, Saint Kevin entered into "the network of eternal life" now. Thus the poet runs down the ways of losing self in the "agony" that is stiff-armed, gone numb, seemingly endless.

Forgive me. I'm a sucker for the subject matter. Though profoundly, happily lapsed, I was born and raised Catholic, as was Seamus Heaney. His Northern Ireland, his outskirts of Derry—of course, very different from the northwest end of Chicago and my parish school. But maybe this in our childhoods was similar: a fascination with saints and their fabulous exploits, often so crazy you'd be on safer ground believing you could fly or really were a foundling from Mars. That said, I never had a Saint Kevin in my cherished hoard of holy cards, collected after funerals for strangers, left in the pews as one bookmark too many. My loss, since his story that drives Heaney's poem is so visually memorable, an outrageous fantasy, a made-for-TV movie (à la the fifth century) in spite of its excruciatingly slow motion and simple plot. Just try keeping your own hand out steady and long enough—days, weeks—for a clutch of blackbird eggs to hatch there, as it's claimed Kevin did. One word: insane. Or, at least, impossible. But in poems, as in myth or one's highest hopes for the highest good—who knows?

Meanwhile, out of that questionable, quirky narrative comes this straightforward poem, managed in two acts, two movements, the first cast in a tale-telling mode from the start. "And then there was . . ." So the Irish legend unfolds and we get the hot skinny on the scene set in Glendalough: the saint's cell, his position (kneeling), how it all plays out in Kevin's open hand—cast *close third-person* in fiction-writer parlance—where the blackbird alights, her "small breast," her "tucked / Neat head and claws," her "warm eggs" recalled in full omniscience. And the saint "moved to pity."

Thus we get the overview, and a zoomed-in camera into Kevin's very heart. Period, paragraph, as my mother would have said, sufficiently fond of saints though she never read or trusted poems much.

This is tricky, I think. Fully underway and however apocryphal, the story's culled, rounded and rounded up, the outside edges rallied to clarify action, then inside for whatever secret self to *mean* rather blatantly. So goes the prose of this poem. And its happily-ever-after, just so. But the unsaid—that great stillness—is having a moment. It's the wait duly inscribed into the narrative by the section break, its little asterisk held up, *stop!* This small formal device seems to anticipate things still puzzling the poet. We know the story, but our lot is to worry legend. And with any luck, get past the knee-jerk proverbial.

The truth is that Heaney is about to open himself to the genuine lyric mystery involved, to the *poetry* therein. And the barebones shape of the piece, the progression of thought—including its break from thought—shows how it all comes up from inner space.

That section break is a held breath between two surges of words, as if Heaney is mulling things over before going back in, this time to tell *and* show. We're down to zero, to *as it happens* after such white space, pause, the emphatic starry dingbat of silence. By now the village explainer has dissolved. The default of rambling sentences in the first section (three!) threaded down through the lines is broken. Ditto the reliance on the predigested, trumpeting declarative. Because really, how to absorb the miraculous?

Syntax has all sorts of weird ideas. Syntax morphs into its various contortions long and short to *reveal*—attitude and sense and what kind of human attention is at stake. Here the poem goes tentative, full of hesitation and honest-to-god questioning, delivered with the triggering pretense of a quasi-reasonable shrug in that next section's first stanza, to raise the gates so the power of image doesn't blow up the border crossing.

> And since the whole thing's imagined anyhow,
> Imagine being Kevin . . .

*Anyhow.* This shift to the "well, whatever" vernacular adds charm and interiority; it turns the discourse from certainty, saves it from the all-knowing adult-voice of the first section. The nature of the question itself sets the formerly self-assured speaker back on his thumbs. He wonders specifically about the body, the misery of poor Kevin's frozen posture for weeks and weeks—"Are his fingers sleeping? Does he still feel his knees?"—until we're also caught up in the exhausting flesh-and-blood details. Just what *would* that feel like?

But questions *insist* that we imagine—that we enter the immediate realm of thinking all this quite real. More unsettling, to grab us, is Heaney asking deeper—"Or has the shut-eyed blank of underearth // Crept up through him?" With one word—*underearth*, apparently invented by the poet for this occasion—everything shifts to a stranger depth. That "underearth" is a little scary. No longer plain physical distress in the making, not simple humility either.

What I mean is: How long have we been here, wandering around this fast-becoming-eternal of the poem? Translation: How long have we been in the world we thought we understood? No matter. Because Heaney is already on to his real territory, where Kevin's state of mind to mindlessness means

> Alone and mirrored clear in love's deep river,
> 'To labour and not to seek reward,' he prays, . . .

Enter more white space, a brief, silent hovering between tercets, that most unstable of seemingly orderly stanzaic pooling. Then a final stab, borrowed off the first section's assertive mode, to define Kevin's pity and patience and weeks of unearthly focus as *forgotten, forgotten, forgotten* the self, the blackbird, even "on the riverbank (he's) forgotten the river's name."

To my ear, this is beyond lovely into hardcore true, each repetition of "forgotten" dropped and picked up so one keeps erasing how we got there, a slight-of-hand that mimes generosity itself. A certain kind of emptiness as good, maybe the best. Surely this kind, where at the river even one's claim to know the river's name disappears. Which is love. Love!—of course. Here, at the poem's end, rarely has that powerful reason to be or do been so delicately, aptly, and surprisingly evoked.

Most moral tales are stupid. This one is not. It may be relevant to add that Seamus Heaney drew on the legend of Saint Kevin in his 1995 Nobel lecture, where his *anyhow* turns up again: "Anyhow, as Kevin knelt and prayed, a blackbird mistook his outstretched hand for some kind of roost . . ." There, eggs finally hatched into fledglings, the poet told his audience in Stockholm, "true to life, if subversive of common sense, at the intersection of natural process and the glimpsed ideal, at one and the same time a signpost and a reminder."

Is that not great? *Subversive, glimpsed, common sense, reminder*: always those few poems worth reading with wonder. And for those of us who keep writing, plugging away toward the art of it—toward all of the above, I tell myself. But my favorites unlock metaphor: here, the odd, hopeful, matter-of-fact miscalculation at the core, that the bird *mistook* the hand, how Kevin knew exactly, waiting anyway for weeks to aid and abet a transformation that might—or might never—come.

# HOW TO DISSECT A CADAVER

It sounds normal enough when put in an ordinary sentence. In the fall semester, 2008, I was given the privilege of participating in Gross Human Anatomy, a class for first-year students in Indiana University's Medical School, its branch at Purdue University where I'd been teaching in the English department for years. I also took Life Drawing in the art department on alternate days ("bodies dead and alive," I lamely joked), both courses the result of a Faculty Fellowship in the Study of a Second Discipline, putting myself into the strangest situation just to see what would happen.

The award was lucky and troubling, especially the go-ahead nod to be a loose cannon in the so-called cadaver lab. I dutifully slipped on the blue scrubs and lab coat they issued me and tried for the calm and X-ray vision required. Every day after class, I did what I've never done: I wrote in a journal. At home—and not exactly in the "tranquility" William Wordsworth advised—I elaborated in my notebook on all I'd observed those earlier hours among the unnerving sights, scents, and sounds around the four cadavers, the focus of the class. I had no idea what might come of these images, these musings into heaven-knows-what.

Eventually a sequence of thirty-two poems (and what turned out to be the title poem of my eighth collection), "Cadaver, Speak" launched me into a new way to work with and beyond my usual method of going blank then taking up whatever wandered to mind. It turned out to be far more willful, given the vast amount of observation and plain time-on-the-wheel involved.

In spring, the poems began. At first, the "speaker" in the cadaver lab—some standardized, poeticized version of me, of course—eked automatically into voice, to hold forth. But it got old—the poet/speaker overthinking yet again: elevated, self-absorbed unto unctuousness, no chance for genuine discovery. Other options? I've rarely trusted persona poems. But I'd been drawn to, most moved by, the oldest cadaver—who was small as my beloved grandmother had been small, that stranger at first lying curled on her side, seeming to sleep in the same way my grandmother had when I was a child looking into her room through the hallway door.

The dismantling of fellow humans to train doctors—well, that's the thing. But what about me, dumbfounded, a clear imposter in my real lab coat? The pure gall of it. Even my favorite cadaver would have disdained, not liked me at all, I was sure. In any case, I saw the same old, same old *I-am-the-poet-and-you're-not* creeping into those early few pieces, that know-it-all rush and, with it, boredom. Which is, alas, rarely a rush.

The revolution in my process turned sharply, on one pronoun. The original version led off with this sentence:

*The body—before they opened her—the darkest dark / must live in there.*

I read and reread, gearing up to move into the poem, whatever shape it might take. Meanwhile, my cadaver, *her* once-among-us very lively indeed, close, wanting in. I suddenly heard this—

*. . . before they opened . . . before they opened ME—*

Yes! *Her* wonder, not mine, at what mysteries would befall *her* in the lab, the cadaver herself talking to the world.

It scared me—not to death, but certainly that fearful surge would keep this going for real. At last, I had a chance to be curious. Let her think thoughts. I, who knew nothing, had no clue.

How to dissect a cadaver? We write to find out.

The sequence took shape, pretty much a flood then, poem after poem, bits of life I kept overhearing, the remembered from my notes and the imagined in my head. Though I was never told anything beyond her age or cause of death, she did open, unaccountably, to charm and darken me: her sorrow, her wit, her tenderness, her humility, her steel. (So that's why fiction writers fall in love with their characters, I suddenly realized, and don't want to leave them, even for an hour, to eat supper . . .)

Try for invisible, I told the self I had, which must mean: be tactful, go empty as possible into poems waiting to be written. Go right now. You can't always count on their patience.

# OH NO

⌣

Because past the angel at the gate, deep into the archive of the humanly possible, it's just that *oh* can turn like that, go under, straight into poetry.

Here's the god's honest: A moment of calm recently came to me, so close to sleep it was sleep. In my dream, I saw a girl whose dark T-shirt read: *All is failure*. Except "failure" was misspelled—part of the dream, too—either "far-lure" or "fear-lure." The words blur. But thank you, whatever sent that.

Because now, I accept *far* or *fear* as the real f-words, both part of *lure* and—most of all—that F as *failure*, as in *All is failure*, a triumph. I hands-down love that, everything *made* of failure, triggered *first* by failure, seen in its light, *built*—at least poetry often is—by one first failed turn of phrase after another, stanzas and more stanzas in a standing pool of white space until a serious full draft lies there, flat.

Failure as blank check and ice floe into inner space. Is this what it is to see clearly?

——

When Sylvia Plath wrote her poem "Poppies in July," in the brilliant frightening throes of her last year on the planet, it underwent surgery, a savaging. An early stab at it meant four couplets, eventually the completed draft morphing to seven with an ending one-liner for good measure, perhaps really managed in a single day: July 20, 1962. So the date on the published version we know suggests—and legend fixes to a stillness. But that day of its making was full of brilliant changes for the poem. Always though, it was direct address, an I–Thou exchange between speaker and flowers, the human and the natural world, and going more and more vulnerable via the questions posed.

A major one from the start goes straightaway into danger: "Little poppies, / Do you do no harm?" she writes in version one, her curiosity morphing to exhaustion, and an ache for its "opiates," and an *if only* moment for release. So we have a kind of overture but then Plath dives deeper, filling in the blanks.

That the poppies, line one in the final draft, evoke hell and fire begins to feel like classic Plath, opening that door neither she nor most of us would want to enter willingly. But she must, and does as even the title grows more specific—not merely "Poppies" but "Poppies in July," the month of searing temperatures and discomfort. Enter the human mouth, red as the poppies. Enter, via metaphor, the risk of marriage. Hold that thought.

Here are the more formal stats. What Plath kept of the poem from its start: the couplet business, two questions, four complete lines, present tense, first person, a steady direct address to the poppies, the hesitant, darkly wondering "if," though it multiplies later. What did *not* stay: an early draft's stalling ellipsis mid-poem that wings pointedly off into outer or inner space ("I cannot touch you. / And it exhausts me to watch you . . .") and her laser focus on the poppies only, the wish to hit and run (just eight lines), her leaving it right there.

But the poppies—didn't they always seem predictable little creatures, at first diminutive, sweet even, to be directly addressed as such? They become "flames" that keep "flickering" and later—abruptly—"Little bloody skirts!" She in fact *exclaims* this, a genuine discovery, beyond observation. It's a shock, however whimsical this surreal metaphor might seem for a second. Then, more—"A mouth just bloodied." Her zoom-lens focus on the body is moving and horrific because to circle the mouth is an absence, a longing too terrible to witness. And so the pain is doubled because we want to look away.

I do the down-home research and turn on my own stove's front burner and stare, its flame truly an alien element. Plath was accurate, a most crazy flickering, "wrinkly and clear red." In the poem's final version (which appeared in the *Ariel* edited by Ted Hughes in 1965 and not in the poet's original plan for the book—for whatever reason—only the less edgy but barbed "Poppies in October"), the image hits bottom to refire. Like I said, not just "little flames" anymore but "little hell flames," she calls them. Her meticulous build of *poem*: miniature time machine of throb and survival. A slow panic that—springs! It does spring. Inward. Toward the end, two *ifs* (if only!) emerge. Those passionate exclamations make the heart-stopping sixth couplet:

> If I could bleed, or sleep!—
> If my mouth could marry a hurt like that!

But she hadn't finished. Not yet. Something close to Gerard Manley Hopkins's ecstatic dark must have kept her going, a deep-ocean despair. One follows back a keening, history's first lament even before there *was* history. If only the poppies' "liquors" might "seep to me . . . / Dulling and stilling," she adds, their dangerous noncolor a pure oblivion. Her actual ending incantation that those liquors "seep to me"—I almost hear it as "come to me"—is weirdly barbed and transforming. Hypnotic. Hallucinatory.

Few poets nearing the edge of melodrama this effectively resist the empty pleasure of its self-indulgent warmth. So austere of Plath, and deeply strange, to use the part and not the whole, her vision deepened by that, the universal delivered via seemingly simple decisions, the choice of an article, for instance—"*the* skin of a mouth," or "*a* mouth just bloodied" and not the expected possessive—"my mouth." Certainly the word "marry" brings up a chilling biographical reference even as it avoids self-pity. No poet was more of a genius with metaphor, such pitch-perfect leap and transformation. No *artist*, I want to say.

"I had a terror—since September," Dickinson wrote a century earlier to Thomas Wentworth Higginson, editor of the *Atlantic Monthly*, "—I could tell to none—and so I sing, as the Boy does by the Burying Ground—"

To go through the eye of a needle, to sew from each end a coherent misery and revelation: others have done such a thing. And some, like Plath, abruptly and brutally *stopped* doing, not only poetry but their lives with it. Yet surely those few went as long as they did because that doing kept them here. Until it didn't.

Ask John Berryman, who leapt to his end, but before? It was *no, no, no, hell no* which really meant *yes.* "I set up *The Dream Songs* as hostile to every visible tendency in American and English poetry—in as far as the English have any poetry nowadays." His words, as he accepted the National Book Award in 1969. "Long poems need gall," he added, "the outrageous, the intolerable—and they need it again and again. The prospect of ignominious failure must haunt them continually." Just so, wild beloved lines of Berryman's #14 in *The Dream Songs* keep coming back. He famously begins "Life, friends, is boring . . ." before winging off by way of lightning strikes and tidal surge, on through the damning, endlessly redundant advice of his mother, to wit: "Ever to confess you're bored / means you have no / Inner Resources" (note Berryman's jubilant caps for those last schoolmarm words!). Of course, the poet comes down hard, deciding (regretfully? triumphantly?) that "I have no / inner resources, because I am heavy bored . . ." And the objects of this boredom? "Peoples" plus "literature, especially great literature . . ."

Gall? Yes. Outrageous, sure. Smart, wily, sad, comic—but "intolerable"? No way.

As for British poetry, in spite of Berryman's blithe dismissal of so much, there's the rediscovered (and republished by Bloodaxe) Rosemary Tonks who walked away, too, though not as suddenly as Plath or Berryman. Tonks, growing silent, frail, nearly blind, hearing voices of Satan, then—but only through birdsong—God himself. This poet disappeared in the 1970s and shuttered herself apart from family and neighbors for years before her death in 2014; it's a private, fully disturbing story. But the work! Chosen by Philip Larkin—no stranger to darkness himself—for his 1973 *Oxford Book of Twentieth-Century English Verse*, her "Story of a Hotel Room" begins "Thinking we were safe—insanity!" And then the love made though they were "Idiots to trust the little hotel bedroom . . ."

More to this, of course. The dark, the "gloom" as "we set about acquiring one another / Urgently! But on a temporary basis as guests." Is there a happy ending?

Threat lies here, in wait, as if she could hear and see some huge meteorite speeding toward Earth. Still, "If the act is clean, authentic, sumptuous / The concurring deep love of the heart / Follows the naked work, profoundly moved by it." As with Plath, this poet's questions and exclamations keep the voice human and grounded in a lyric progression of place, evening, an intimacy, a not-quite regret. And there's her brilliant redefinition, sex as "the naked work" or as "acquiring one another / Urgently! But on a temporary basis / Only as guests . . ." Nevertheless one can be "profoundly moved by it." Her subtle mix of decorum and nerve and abandon: no wonder Larkin chose Tonks's poem—Philip Larkin of "They fuck you up, your mum and dad / They don't mean to / but they do. . . ." Berryman, back at that National Book Award ceremony, added this insistence to his brief remarks: "It is no good looking for models. We want antimodels." Which is to say, *unlike* engenders *like*, some *disconnect* deep enough to *connect*, regardless of risk.

Again and again, past the angel at that gate, it's back to the mythic garden in spite of its dangers, a first forbidden bite, what for years I've called "bummer lit," what we must half-love, the complexity, the pull toward *something truly bad has happened, is happening, will happen.* Therefore we write, therefore *literature* present and to come. In this, we resemble our lost betters—Dickinson, Keats, Milton, William Blake—and back to the first cave dweller sick at heart over the loss of the one bloodthirsty Vandal buddy who was bearable, even treasured, and so belted out the first elegy. *Oh no.* The ache for a tangled, gleaming thread. Add to the great subjects of poetry— time, death, knowledge, love—a human hopelessness, worlds lost or almost, and our perennial individual fuck-ups. And, right from the start, the seductive failure of poetry, its slim-and-none chance to solve anything at all.

Because, like scientists, poets learn to follow this by heart: whatever *does not compute.* Small eventually gets big, and big small enough for the page. And, always, there's the charm bracelet of *only trouble is interesting* that fiction writer Janet Burroway famously forged but which belongs to poetry, too. Failure, reasonably enough, never fails. Failure we do naturally, and do and redo and is done to us. We're sad experts at it.

———

Which is why I've become Coleridge's obsessive wedding guest, telling and retelling how I once stopped by my public library to send a quick email. Two terminals down, a dapper-looking young man kept talking (through Skype, I supposed) to—was it really the Pentagon? He said his full name, politely asked that it be repeated before distinctly reporting what he called sexual abuse via radiation aimed from afar at his "private parts." Would those at the Pentagon find the culprit immediately? He'd be grateful, he said. Where are you calling from?—I imagined a voice at the other end careful, asking this a second time. Because he first gave stark "coordinates" via latitude and longitude. Then again, his request that his words be repeated as if this this were a seagoing vessel far from shore, contact uncertain, possibly shattered by wind and rain, all adrift in a random earnest wash and moan. At my screen, my doing e-whatever vanished. The truth is: all stopped in me as I faked otherwise.

Poetry, or—what isn't like this? The scary at-odds just under the surface. Probably in all of us. Always a glimpse of that.

I had no right to listen. My *glued-to-it-anyway* set me up as an intimate, aware of him, concerned for him. And for those dealing with his desperation in the badly paid, phone-answering lowest ranks of the Pentagon—feeling for them, too. How often are we stricken by how close our own madness lies, our fears so easily amplified, gone surreal, overwhelming, toxic? Those ten minutes in the library abruptly offered up a skewed looming world. I kept at it: analogy, analogy, fortune, fate, this guy, my own life, any of us, all of us.

Consider the many things (X times Z equals thousands) with this same dire soundtrack, *oh no, oh no, oh no*: certain elections and their appalling aftermath; what the doctor might tell you by way of a strip of reckless lines on graph paper from the heart that reads like bad atonal music; poem after poem aching to come through us; a phone ringing and ringing and no, you don't pick it up.

In that library, its blessed widening orbit of mind, I froze in my seat: Aren't we all the saddest, richest, most many-layered failed creatures possible? My own Venn diagram of sanity just barely crossing and containing my derailment, I looked on, pretending to take in stride whatever comes. No way around it, I was—*am*—a citizen of this peculiar human race.

And poetry—everything to do with that.

# IN THE MIDDLE OF EVEN THIS

—

A year before COVID-19 became a threat and then an ongoing dark obsession, the world passed the one-hundredth anniversary of the so-called Spanish flu pandemic. Mostly it was scientists and medical researchers who noted the 1918 outbreak as a history-shaping event. But pandemics raise vital questions for those of us who write, such as, *How can poets take on the worldly and the terrible without forsaking passionate human connection?* More to the point, *How do poets make major, universal events personally matter at the flesh-and-bone level?* Certain historical eras—consider Trump's, made of smoke and fog— force real urgency onto such questions. And an epidemic is *made* of flesh and bone, after all. Still, like most writers, I think toward examples.

*Kyrie,* I'd blurt out. Ellen Bryant Voigt's rich, varied sequence of poems published in 1995 about the 1918 pandemic is one of the crucial books written in my lifetime—moving, unnerving, clear-eyed brilliant—and, I fear, prophetic. Far away, and as close as *right this minute.*

It's also my favorite. For a long time now I've been claiming it as such. The collection darkly charms and disturbs. It was a vast surprise, too, how the book came to be. I learned this in an airport in the early 1990s, walking with the poet before we went separate ways to catch our flights, my hearing for the first time of her honest-to-god *research.* (She finger-quoted that word, but not to shrug it off.) Did I

52

know the flu epidemic of those years killed off a third of the population in some towns? In America, in Europe. And hit the trenches of WWI hard? I had to start thinking "like a novelist," she said later. I'd add to that: an historian, a witness, a soothsayer, a broken and shattered citizen of the world (though not without some hope). Which is lyric, by the way—as everlasting as lament.

Case closed. Cause and effect. But not only.

I mean, what to do with a chain of real events, with *narrative*, that impulse that seems to make so many poets queasy now, open to the charge of (god forbid) being *old-fashioned*. But poetry isn't a fashion. I recall a remark made by Voigt in a discussion at Warren Wilson's MFA program where I've taught for years, her trademark reasonable passion flaring up: *my friends, we are all lyric poets!* I imagine she mostly meant what she calls the "dramatic lyric," the drama drawn from a profound sense of story, the treacherous human on-and-on, its shards and leaps of synapse and wrong turns made within a grounded, steely feel for concrete imagery that I've for decades called the "beloved particulars." These particulars keep the lyric impulse from drifting off into la-la land, the abstract, the ultra-cryptic and the too-precious. Then there's poetry's infamous self-absorption, which can give it a very bad name indeed.

None of that nonsense for Ellen Voigt. Still, "our lives for it," as Frost wrote more than half a century ago. Dream as unsentimental dream. Detail that *means*, beyond clever stage-setting. "Have you heard a dead man sigh? / A privilege, that conversation," she says in the middle of the carnage the flu epidemic left behind, bodies so altered that no gravedigger could tell who was Black and who was not.

Poetry strikes me, then, as that huge privilege—the site of many conversations between the reader and a speaker, there to pivot, to keep track, to question, to give context. In *Kyrie*, we see a method that borrows from the playwright; overheard voices rage or cast their asides so poignantly we can hardly bear them. Which is to say, the persona poem lives in this book—the doctor, the soldier, the teacher holding forth to themselves or others or to the world, as if asked: *say your piece, then*. I sometimes think of it as "peace," the reverse of war offered up as a break in violence, a solace, an urgent and private—if very dark—reconsidering before the next public assault.

Peace, then, because in this book of global distress and formal battle what its characters say of their dreams and their days carries a kind of luck regardless. We hear their voices in a kind of eternal zone outside of time where poetry does live as austere, torn, stubbornly mortal. As befits someone first trained as a pianist, Voigt is a poet with an uncanny ear. "I always need a line, a snatch of music, to start a poem," she has written, "and with the fixed circumstance (of that book), I started hearing more and more lines—'Oh yes, I used to pray'—and then would figure out who might have said that." Given the dire context, it doesn't take much to catch the ominous, ironic edge in that *Oh yes*—

I've brought *Kyrie* several times before my students. Once, in the middle of the term with an undergraduate class, I emailed the poet about her methods. My charges had questions: Why the war *and* the flu—an unthinkable double whammy? How did these particular characters (teacher, doctor, soldier, etc.) get in there in the first place? What about her use of epistolary form, the letters that the soldier writes from the trenches? I wondered the obvious: her riveting of narrative and lyric, the collection's overall design, and her reason—given her Protestant upbringing—for the book's title, drawn from the phrase *kyrie eleison*, chanted right before the offertory, as I remember, the only moment of Greek in the Latin Mass. A plea meaning *Lord*—as in *Lord, have mercy*, an ache for sense and forgiveness against *How fast and far can I run from the world's and my own nightmares?*

In her email, Voigt wrote that she wanted something different after her 1988 collection *The Lotus Flowers*, and this desire triggered "some sort of anti-narrative fit," fragments that would, in part, become her fourth book, *Two Trees*. "I told myself to think as a painter would," she continued. "Monet painted the same haystacks over and over, each time in a different light. For a poet, what's the equivalent of light? Tone, I think." After that particular collection, she realized which tone was missing: irony. And "being such an earnest person," as she put it, she chose a country doctor as her first speaker, similar to the one who had practiced in the rural Virginia of her childhood, "someone," she said, "whose life circumstances were such that irony was imperative to survival, to coping, to staying sane."

Can I repeat that and let it land again, slowly? In the face of dire "life circumstances" there's an irony *imperative to survival, to coping, to staying sane.* (So it is I watched Stephen Colbert every night in the Trump era, I suddenly realize, just to hang on.)

The notion of sanity—how rare is that, especially these days? How *Ellen Voigt* is that, one might say. Though an autobiographical thread triggers this work—the stricken boy beside the bed already mourning his mother is based on the experience of her own orphaned father— the poems move beyond their imagined time and place because, conversely, they honor actual experience. The doctor in *Kyrie*, for instance, reliably turns up on horseback in the fevered duration of this national calamity, house to house. His small soliloquies pin down a near-unbearable run through sickness and loss. His exhaustion mirrors the state of mind of so many in the hard lockjaw of this book, the national and world tragedy it evokes—the various speakers in whom we see our current terrors, not in the shadows anymore.

The doctor supplies a tireless grace as well. We *might* survive. We *might*, though as readers or writers, what to do with our own desperation beyond picturing the worst? One option: do that, regardless.

> . . . deep in the lungs a cloudiness not clearing;
>       vertigo, nausea, slowed heart, thick green catarrh,
> nosebleeds spewing blood across the room—

Soon the doctor's bag is empty, the one he "carried like a Bible." He shares "a jug of homemade corn" with the "whole fevered family [who] lay head to foot in their own and others' filth . . ."

Still, how much can we endure and what's the dosage, the cure? In a book-length sequence particularly, architecture clarifies. Voigt considers *Kyrie* one long poem though she has called its staggered build a series of "loose sonnets," choosing that form for its "necessary pathos" and to give each speaker "equal time at the mic." Her small-town characters who bar the house against the flu and, lacking a lamb, streak the door with the blood of a cat to ward off pestilence—or her soldiers in the trenches of WWI who lose limbs, have nicknames, eat chess pie, wear handwoven scarves made by a beloved—are burdened by despair and appalling premonitions but shards of desire and possibility too, though not many. Poetry needs realists.

Sweet are the songs of bitterness and blame,
against strangers spitting on the street,
the neighbor's shared contaminated meal,
the rusted nail, the doctor come too late.

In an essay somewhere, Tony Hoagland wrote that shifts in tone
are the real narrative of a poem. I'd add that such angling makes it
feel true, taking whatever's happening on the surface *underground*, to
the deepest human interior, to the only place that's trustworthy; tone
itself shades progression in the poem, a factual and emotive advance
and retreat, a circling that nevertheless ends, the light on Monet's
haystacks that tells us time has been there: summer, fall, winter,
spring. *It must change*, and with that, Wallace Stevens advises us on
how the architecture of memorable poetry works.

One formal word for that change, that rupture, is *volta*, which can
be anywhere in a sonnet's small-page geography. ("Why not, I figured, put the couplet in the middle?" Voigt asked in a parenthetical,
in her reply to my email.) As for her thinking "like a novelist," it's not
one but two stories, always, to register and balance—what's *out there*
and *in here*. For *Kyrie*, it's the war at home, so to speak (via village and
school, barnyard, sickroom) against the one in Europe taking many
thousands of lives with it, including those in the trenches. The poet
makes it immediate for those of us in the future who can only imagine how this happened.

But it's complex. And takes a while. "I had to think back, up to
*before* the crisis and *extend past* the crisis," Voigt added.

The fact is we're drawn to poetry because its great subjects really
*are* great—knowledge, time, beauty, death, love. *Kyrie* is one book
that taps narrative design and energy to bring these subjects to lyric
life. Yet how often are we as writers and readers haunted—that is,
outright *gifted* from some dark—and lifted into a communal shared
idea and image. Then, as individuals, we're reinvented and write what
we write. It's dangerous. Thrilling. Terrible.

Our own grossly ignoble era requires this. Am I pitching a greater
ambition here? I hope not, or not exactly. We begin in silence. Then, a
voice comes and one picks it up like tuning in short wave, an alert or
a warning that's otherwise lost under the static.

Pleasure's there in the making too. That's the survival guide, the hope part. "I was writing the *Kyrie* poems in my sleep," Ellen Voigt told me in that long-ago email. "And isn't that the *best?*" she said. "Isn't that what we live for?—not the finished poems, but right at the living heart of their unfolding."

# MELODRAMA

‿

Which gets a bad rap. My son tells me something I never knew before. It's a musical term. It means opera, first of all: a story set to music, a *drama* carried by *melo*, song. *Mom, don't get your knickers in a twist over this again*, he implies as I hold the landline receiver close to my ear. Long-distance, we used to say about such phone calls. I imagine him singing the *get over it* I hear in his tone, maybe in his regular voice or in playful falsetto, our once mock-doing *La Bohème* in the kitchen, staging the simplest request in D-minor:

> Oh please, please! Take out the compost!
> Okay, okay! I see it overrunneth!

But—seriously? It's just that melodrama has always worried me. What about the standard bad stuff always about to happen in opera, I argue, the raised hands as exclamation points, the collective choral shriek of onlookers, the hit-the-lights plunge into dark after the shiny knife goes down? Be fair, my son says. Then it could be we're both thinking of those subtle duets, gradual and intricate, how they tear your heart, ending abruptly before you expect—*Bohème*'s Mimi wrapped in Rudolfo's arms, *The Consul*'s Magda mournfully interrupting her husband John, or the tomb-with-a-view finale (as my brother calls it) between Aida and Radames—all the lush, various stops and starts from Puccini, Menotti, Verdi. And big, this tangle always so earnest, such grand and charged dignity to whatever ordinary or outrageous shard of word or deed, a grave eternal eye on whatever mess we've made—or will make. In the body, the very sound exhausts and thrills.

Familiar pathways the nerve finds through muscle, the electrical charge of realizing anything crucial: Are we so predictable a creature that we all *cave* the same way? How a sonnet has some opening jab, heartbeat unto argument, then a turn, a new way to see, a winnowing and an arrival echoed ever since in free verse. Is our brain so used to this that it's become theater? Or consider Freytag's Pyramid—the guy, not surprisingly, a nineteenth-century drama critic—and how it freezes narrative into formula, his triangle drawn on the board by English teachers a million times, a dream for our next step and the next nicked from Aristotle: the rising until *get the point?* falling slow or fast, at an angle. That's another *get over it*, meaning something actually to get over and get on with, I suppose, an honest-to-god human fate that takes an hour, a day, years. Who cares if you know what will happen—the waterfall of sorrow's same old, of boredom's deliberate silence pushing off into another way to notice.

Or to remember. For instance, from Dickinson's slush pile, a torn notebook page photographed for that Michigan book, *Open Folios.* After ED's few words about a tree in winter, she writes in her terrible cursive:

> I never heard
> you call anything
> beautiful before—
> It remained
> with me

Not the tree but the *telling* keeps ringing in the ear: "remained / with me." It makes a shape.

Perhaps what we do, our movement through time, *is* musical—it repeats, repeats—therefore is *melo*, is *drama*. One hears it linked like singing links, one note, slight breath before another, voice next to voice in whisper or resistance. No filter. Sound enters the body any which way, the ear an indifferent machine, little incus and malleus and stapes in there, merging, making sense of whatever onslaught. Its hunger is huge. High contrast, cause and effect, loud, soft, the edges sharp. Something happens. It sings to us, or we sing *it* to the world that goes on, open to us or not. What was that that Elizabeth Bishop said in a conversation once recalled in the *Antioch Review* by Wesley Wehr? That we always reveal the truth about ourselves ". . . despite ourselves. It's just, quite often, we don't like how it turns out." A given then: melodrama lurks behind any story, pattern, poem. It's like a virus, always in the air. And some of us succumb.

To succumb. That includes a lot but what about my rage at the feel-good end of some hokey movie? *So melodramatic!* we say, the punch of it, a few tears coming despite the manipulation. Are we so predictably hot-wired? Really? *Mea culpa, mea culpa, mea maxima culpa*, from the old Latin Mass: "through my fault, through my fault, through my most grievous fault." Tears! How is it the body *knows* in spite of good sense and taste, in plain dogged embarrassment, releasing them regardless? Take that, oh fine cool aesthetic, sophisticated mind with its perfect engineering.

To be moved. *Moved.* I love that word, how it happens *to* you, a surprise, a kind of miraculous undoing about which Gerard Manley Hopkins wrote in his journal: ". . . there is always one touch, something striking sideways and unlooked for . . . and this may be so delicate that the pathos seems to have gone directly to the body and cleared the understanding in its passage . . ." *Delicate* isn't exactly how to get at the not so sleight-of-hand of melodrama. But a little wallowing in the theater's large dark can't be that bad, can it?

Meanwhile, this delicate meanwhile: Elizabeth Bishop's greatest hit, "One Art," a model of reserve and passion and wit, plus a terrible—however brief—altogether human realization. Her poem is a courtly, careful mash-up, the unsaid speaking as clearly as what actually makes it to the page. Irony, after all, orbits the wink-wink-nod-nod of the unspoken, a secret life that's semi-obvious, delicious to share.

"One Art" is an immediate pleasure via Bishop's colloquial ease, however measured its villanelle givens of obsessive repetition. Her well-known refrain—*The art of losing isn't hard to master*—comes right off the bat, first line and already tongue-in-cheek, a staged shrug about beloved things in peril, disappearing. Though she starts comic and small-scale—with keys, an "hour badly spent"—as in any *practice* to learn a great art, the losses quickly morph into a more weighted personal mode: "my mother's watch" vanished, and loved houses (three of them)! Then she's going larger, unto global: *rivers, realms, a continent.*

"I miss them, but it wasn't a disaster."

But all "hard to master," such losses, partly whimsical by way of simple geography, wild leaps, and a bird's migratory, exacting eye until the final move inward that really does switch, click, get down, get close, never to be saved by casual humor or anything else. "Even losing you (the joking voice, a gesture / I love) I shan't have lied."

Her characteristic steel won't belabor this vulnerable moment, won't and can't—"It's evident / the art of losing's not too hard to master," Bishop re-insists after her revealing slip. But we get a stained new thought: "though it may look like (*Write* it!) like disaster," she says, in fact, *writing* that, ending the poem in a quickened second twist of that screwdriver parenthetical.

Her "*write* it"—old Anglo-Saxon's mono-stress emphatic—goes on, secret and regardless and of course as lifeline, way beyond the poem. And then there's that wrenching do-it-anyway hit of italics. Here it's grief in this momentary dive under the surface where loss *looks like*, probably is "like disaster," a greater dark now that even the soothing rhyme against the predictable "master" can't fix, though getting back to work must be a kind of solace. It's a villanelle, for god's sake; you have to forge on—write it!—repeat, to end only this way. That does cut short the release of tears, a sudden *almost* bit of melodrama in its wake. Could that be as haunting as the one-thousand-foot spread of watery lurch and undertow any ocean liner worth its tonnage leaves behind, that wake?

What we think of as the first draft of Bishop's poem, then titled "How to Lose Things" or "The Gift of Losing Things" or "The Art of Losing Things"—from Vassar's archives—might be such a wake; that early version does seep back. On her old manual machine, she typed a very sprawling attempt, notes really, including this on the list of lost things—

A piece of one continent—
and one entire continent. All gone, gone forever and ever . . .

Out of the would-be penultimate stanza, this did not survive—

One might think this would have prepared me
one average-sized not ~~especially~~ ——— exceptionally
beautiful or dazzlingly intelligent person
(except for blue eyes)(only the eyes <u>were</u> exceptionally
        beautiful and
                        the hands <u>looked</u> intelligent) . . .

In the closing lines adding another disappearance: "another
continent—the whole damned thing!" Then finally:

He who loseth his life, etc.—but he who /
loses his love—never, no never never never again—

Think Verdi, think Puccini. Or be reminded of King Lear's *never,
never, never, never, never!* as Ellen Voigt was when we spoke of it. The
orchestra rising, hands to a collar, a flood of sound from a throat.

Pure melodrama! Though reason's logical build is here, it's because
of melodrama that we have Bishop's lasting, heartbreaking poem—
her numerous drafts wrestled sorrow down to mere mention. Which
is greater, more necessary in this struggle: her witty reserve pressing
hard or that great out-of-control ache that must have started everything? No answer yet. Sincerity and irony still restlessly at it and at it.

Three additional thoughts now—

#1. The Contemporary Museum of Art, Chicago, around 1973,
right before a reading. The poet Paul Carroll is in the audience, the
most generous editor of *The Young American Poets*, an anthology that
meant much to those of us who were still young but also old enough

when it appeared, in 1968—where I discovered Louise Glück, not to mention Charles Simic and James Tate and Ron Padgett, not far from their baby fat. The pre-reading audience chat and buzz narrowed to Roy Lichtenstein, whose massive paintings patched the wall. Everyone around us had something to say.

I recall his campy cartoons, one big weepy female face, her talk balloon blown up to read *It doesn't matter what I say!* while a male face in another painting, equally oversized and looking off as a young woman sulks in the background, speaks into his bubble: *Forget it! Forget me! I'm fed up with your kind.* At these clichés and earnest exaggerations a lively, happy scorn rose up in the room, many living out a similar melodrama in their own young lives of break-up and come back again. At twenty-two, I was among those who pointed and mocked, who made fun of.

Paul Carroll—so much older than us, a large man, impeccable against our fashion-of-the-day ragged jeans, his derby and pin-striped suit, his great charm and goodwill and sadness—went silent for a while before saying: *But that's the way people really talk, isn't it?*

#2. Impossibly beautiful—with all the necessary shadow that claim implies—is Theodore Roethke's poem "The Far Field," from which comes what might be my favorite jump-start first line (and shouldn't this really be on his tombstone?): "I dream of journeys repeatedly." But to tamp that down, there's the "driving alone, without luggage, out a long peninsula" only to stall "Churning in a snowdrift / Until the headlights darken." That's it for the first of five sections, all lush renderings of the natural world, next—"At the field's end . . . Haunt of the cat-bird, nesting-place of the field-mouse" where "among the tin cans, tires, rusted pipes, broken machinery,— / One learned of the eternal." *Eternal.* Thus, high abstraction enters ("the thinky thinky," Roethke called it) to enrich or weigh down. But first, this gorgeous unapologetic countdown of spring delights:

> For to come upon warblers in early May
> Was to forget time and death:
> How they filled the oriole's elm, a twittering restless cloud, all
>     one morning.

The poet goes on, "eyes blurred from the bird shapes . . ." Or later, lines that put us in our rightful place on the planet, the speaker in a "slow river . . . fingering a shell / Thinking: / Once I was like this, mindless. . . ."

On and on this stunning meditation goes, idea to hard detail and back again to arrive midway at this: perhaps the worst, worst, *worst*, most squishy melodramatic phrase in the history of good poetry: "the windy cliffs of forever."

*Huh?* That's what my thought balloon says in the margin, were I to draw one. Granted, he's already jacked up the mood music in the previous line—"I learned not to fear infinity." But it continues to shock me that Roethke *kept on going* into poetry la-la land with this bit of purple prose. "The windy cliffs of forever . . ."! What does it even mean?

My beloved old cousin Elinor had her Achilles heel, known to her worried daughters as her "wheee! factor" which meant she'd spend her savings, spend down to nothing left, if given half a chance. Who knows how that crazy *let-loose* in her, that impulse to pitch it all— caution included—made everything else we miss and cherish about her possible: her wit and warmth, her intolerance of intolerance, her embrace of the world and its weirdness.

In more merciful, if not saner, moments then, I can think: So what? Roethke gave way now and then. But it's brave and it's great. And probably crucial to every fine thing he wrote that he dared that edge.

#3. A couple of words come back, dragging their ghost: *Sylvia Plath*. A single numbing stress begins, then ends, that run of four syllables, and with that name, the terrible last work looms up, late 1962 into the bitter winter of '63, before her death in London that February, her scathing and meticulous attention to the present moment, day after day, that made so many poems in *Ariel*. "Daddy" is among them, its wrath a trademark by now, drowning out the quieter, more compelling parts of Plath's genius. The poem is commonly read as near melodrama, an operatic outburst, an invective against father and husband. Biography has done it in good.

No doubt for compelling reasons. There's a bread-crumb trail of image from life: Plath's difficult father and his German heritage, his position as a professor of entomology squaring with the poem's figure "at the blackboard," his death when she was ten an experience identical to the speaker's. The drafts for the poem, now in the Mortimer Rare Book Room at the Smith College library, show fury imprinted and measured out from the first though the last stanza and its memorable ending utterance—"Daddy, you bastard, I'm through"—was a fiery addendum handwritten into the typed second version, albeit not much different in tone from her famous opening, in place from the start:

> You do not do, you do not do
> Any more, black shoe
> In which I have lived like a foot
> For thirty years, poor and white,
> Barely daring to breathe or Achoo.

Her "Achoo" (capitalized à la A. A. Milne), deliberate and whimsical, might have come from storybook rhymes she'd been reading to her small children. But the *melo* in her drama is heated exclamatory on obsessive repeat. And her drafts for the piece aren't a flipbook; she didn't start slowly and change a lot. Pretty much the poem roars, teeth bared, from the get-go. Still, it's staggering what can happen in the making, the writer remade too, scaring herself until fact itself fades, to get all jacked up via metaphor and analogy to become somehow *truer*. How else to account for the poem's last hammer blow, her final stanza's over-the-top, weirdly animated, medieval folktale–grim lines that proceed her ringing "Daddy . . . I'm through" by way of those murderous near-Lilliputian "villagers" who "never liked you. / . . . dancing and stamping on you. / They always *knew* it was you." That vengeful *you*, the triggering heart of all this. By the end, who was writing that?

Because Plath, to a BBC interviewer, later carefully removes herself. "Here is a poem," she tells him, "spoken by a girl with an Electra complex. Her father died when she thought he was God. Her case is complicated by the fact that her father was also a Nazi." Come again?

Backstory then, poem as case study, a persona piece. Like anyone believes that, says whatever Plath fan/fanatic you choose, passionate young women, mostly, who have just discovered her, a few of them my undergraduate students who stand with me in the hallway after class and fight for her right to be a woman wounded and fierce. They are unaware it was the grounded, dogged artist in her—not the suicide— who made the brilliant work. I respect and honor this artist above all her dark suffering: the completely sane poet within that kept Plath vital and alive as long as possible.

Remote control is still control.

On the BBC, Plath continued, almost dismissive in her acquired British accent, calling "Daddy" an "awful little allegory" spoken by that Nazi's daughter locked in her own terrible twentieth-century moment, a layer that adds weight and historical edge to the piece to change it, and alter our received idea of the poet herself. Had Plath lived, is this mainly—or, at least, first—how we would see her poem?

All these claims and layered *reads*, after the fact. What is the link between art and life? No one knows—even the writer, sometimes— what happens in the night-blind whirlpool of the making.

---

There's this: girls in my grade school collected holy cards, faux-gilt-edged and frozen sentimental pictures of saints, the Sacred Heart, the Virgin Mary hoarded up to vie with our brothers' baseball stash, their cards coming in packs with a hard pink slab of bubble gum in the middle. I had—still have—favorites in my cache. But in my whole childhood, not one Saint Sebastian turned up, every inch of him—minus the skivvied bits—pin-cushioned brightly by arrows, the ultimate martyrdom, Rome, 288 C.E. Was it his near nudity that put the nuns off? Or it may well be the holy card extruders simply played it safe, going for the more sickly-sweet options for the kids and old ladies who would fondly save their handiwork.

A devoted lapsed-Catholic for decades, I might be allowed this one arched-eyebrow thought: Is it not partly the sick genius of the Church that Sebastian is *also* the patron saint of archers? How comic is that? (No waste. Use the whole chicken, I call it.) He's the guardian of soldiers, too, once in the Roman Army himself. Most astonishing and least known: he is the patron saint of surviving the plague.

The fact is—breaking news!—Sebastian *did* outlast those arrows. Proof: at least one painting of Saint Irene lovingly tending his many wounds as he slumps against her in the Vatican Museum. In any case, he healed; he lived to tell the tale. Which is why my husband and I can play *Where's Waldo* to find him, over and over, in museums in Europe—or America, for that matter—room after gallery room of Sebastians in various melodramatic, tormented gyrations, even ridiculously out of place at times, in the lower corner of some large, cozy Nativity, say, Mary and Joseph and a lit baby Jesus basking in cow breath and sheep warmth. There he is, to the right and down, oblivious, practically naked and tangled in rope, feathered arrows starry-haywire, the saint in agony or indifference, depending, but surely foreseeing his recovery, already plotting his return to Rome to mouth off to the emperor and get his dream of proper martyrdom at last; soldiers beat him to death.

But to survive those arrows, that first assault!—a miracle of the first order.

Think of it this way: it's 1349. If Sebastian made it, then certainly his presence in whatever painting *you* commission will shield self and family from the Black Death sweeping the known world, some two hundred million dead before it's over. That's the deal. That *was* the deal—and with it, the Saint Sebastian survivor industry duly cranked up for melodrama, artists both good and only so-so at the ready.

Which is to say, not only does image last, it humbles and over-whelms. It's desperately practical too. Sebastian then, as metaphor and model: a signal, a white flag, a bloodied saint-as-tattoo on some bicep to flash in a fight. Sebastian, a stay against danger, a safety valve, a vaccine, luck's rabbit foot, puppeteer of salvation. You rack up your chips for dear life and shove it all to the center of the table, Sebastian with his zillion arrows a hope-against-hope, a lamb nailed to the door to trick an angel, a stand-alone and cut to the quick but healing in secret regardless, a *so there*, an *in your face*, the held high note in an aria, or the moment in the poem before—beware!—it really gets dark. Sebastian twisting in his corner, or skinny-hogging the whole canvas, a shape toward allegory, larger than life in paint-ing after painting until he's a repeat, repeated to make *melo* this *drama*, the worst of it to best all bad things. A charm. And please, a future.

Poetry knows we are as close as a feather to disaster.

Is it hope then, since she intuited so much? Plath for her BBC inter-view making herself distant, even haughty, certain that in "Daddy" her scarred, giant, triumphant name-calling speaker "has to act out the awful little allegory . . . before she was free of it." *She*. Nice try.

Melodrama: to exaggerate is to get bigger, and so continue, to last a little longer like those butterflies or birds (peacocks, some hawks) whose feathers carry markings to fake huge eyes. It will scare away snakes, or attract a mate.

# FUGUE MOMENTARY

A confession: I have no business writing about Hart Crane. I have a bad history with the guy, once very happily dropping a course in which I was assigned to lead a discussion of *The Bridge*. The truth is I had another reason for bailing out, wanting desperately to get my hands on clay, lose myself in that turning wheel—in short, to take Ceramics, a class which met the same hour. Still, to be released from trying to make sense, in public, of this very puzzling poet was a definite perk and made my decision a wildly thrilling, if cowardly, act. This was graduate school, after all. Though we were writers, not scholars, this sort of thing wasn't done. Poets had to read, and certainly they read poets. One stayed in such a class and diligently absorbed what smoked and burned on the page. One *made* the presentation.

I haven't completely avoided *The Bridge* in the many years since; its ambition alone overwhelms and astonishes. The great Whitman—Crane, his devout defender—lurks there. And I love the near mythic coincidence surrounding its making, that Crane lived overlooking the Brooklyn Bridge of that time, in the same room once rented by Washington Roebling, son of its chief engineer and the one who oversaw its construction for his father from a distance, by telescope, because he was paralyzed by caisson disease. I think about this sometimes, how Crane's friend Waldo Frank claimed the poet discovered this rather enormous detail later, after the fact. Good thing, I always think. Crane was haunted enough.

But perhaps he would have relished knowing this at the time he lived and wrote there—yet another layer to his vision: the vast *idea* of the bridge; then its day-to-day rise and complication, Roebling's quiet, damaged body far off, behind windows, as he watched so closely. Nevertheless, the *lens* of that, the counter lens of the poet who records and figures and assigns weight; the even larger notion, the history of the country drawn in, all of it together, barely—some would say never—melded into a coherent shape for the epic Crane himself called heroic.

Because complexity, expansion, density. These qualities are so characteristic of this poet's work, it seems ham-handed and obvious to mention them. Romantic. Rhetorical. And then add the troubling bits, forever—or perhaps it only seems forever: his sentimentality, his predictable cadence and mannered language, his boosterism for America, for the "Machine Age," his fondness for bombast and excess and prophecy. One begins to give up and close the book all over again, thinking of certain contemporaries, how fresh Williams seems in comparison, how acute and wily Marianne Moore. The perfect gravity in Stevens, or Frost. The passion of Langston Hughes.

Then, no—here and here and over here in *White Buildings* and *The Bridge* and among the pieces he didn't live to gather into another book, this poet can surprise, be inventive and irresistibly strange. Even subtle. Sweet, without too much mist involved. Fierce. Convincing. So the jury's out on the tarmac somewhere and there's a lot of traffic; one can have at least two minds—maybe more—about Hart Crane. Enter the smaller lyric pieces, some of which add far more than they subtract.

Crane's poem "Moment Fugue" is a late work, published in the journal *transition* early in 1929, a year before his collection *The Bridge* appeared. At his death three years later, it was found in the sheaf marked for his next and third book. The Depression hit after the poem's making but "Moment Fugue" is definitely a city piece, weighted with the growing despair of its time. In a way it fits Crane's own requirement worked out in his prose for "poetry in the Machine Age," not so much that it "absorbs" the machine or "climatizes it as . . . casually as trees, cattle, galleons, castles," but in how it underscores what the poet thought crucial for any serious writing in the new century: "an extraordinary capacity for *surrender* [italics his], at least temporarily, to the sensations of urban life."

Hart Crane loved cities, especially New York. But to *surrender* to the city's particulars, by way of "Moment Fugue," must have been an unusually selfless act, the focus of attention out there and elsewhere, several steps away from the more typical lyric poem which honors the first-person speaker's very private orbit in and out of what—often for Crane, at least—can be a calculated and considerable heat. He cautions that such surrender be to "sensations." We're in the realm of the interior, considering *how* to attend to these outward things and the ricochet action they create inside us.

I need to follow that action in "Moment Fugue," as swift and tangled and maddening as anything in Crane's larger works—a kind of microcosm of his anxious, deliberately ballasted style. Crane calls this piece a *fugue*. Fair enough, given the open-ended definitions musicologists offer. Not exactly a form, many say; the fugue is more a process, a practice, a texture. The poet's sentences merge and give up and procrastinate and steal from each other; a lot goes on, often rather quickly. A fugue—why not? The word is from the Latin *fuga*, meaning flight, and from *fugere*, to flee. There are "episodes" involved, the initial one and those that race after with little or very large shifts, "developmental" layers through which the world widens or deepens.

A key to Crane's poem might be the *in stretto* effect of so many fugues, a voice which appears before the one ahead of it has finished, the small resulting cacophony and overlay—as in *logjam*, as in *how-in-the-hell-do-I-get-back-to-the-trailhead?*—entirely prized. But, *texture*. I like the every-which-way woven notion of it. It fits this poet's density of movement, which seems at times without reason, bypassing clear syntax, that old guardian of sense particularly in Crane's generation. Which is to say, there are rules but the urgent weight—or multiplicity—of the cargo can break them.

It's visual art that helps me most with "Moment Fugue." A highly figurative piece, its pressure points are images pure and simple—flowers, a flower seller, the subway newsstand, gestures of buying and selling. One rather violent simile in the otherwise most daily of scenes suggests a narrative briefly, shot down many layers, a seething and a shock. But intense, nearly surreal camerawork is required; one sees with the care and distance of that quick lens.

Little wonder that one of Crane's long-term friends was Walker Evans, who shared his passion for the Brooklyn Bridge, and that they actually met on site, the twenty-four-year-old Evans armed with a six-dollar camera, his first, aiming up at the massive structure when the poet noticed him and called out. It turns out Evans was surprised in all those conversations that followed at how astutely Crane could keep "raving on" about photography. But it was earlier, in a letter to another revered photographer, Alfred Stieglitz, that Crane wrote his most revealing comment on that art. "The eerie speed of the shutter is more adequate than the human eye to remember . . . Speed is at the bottom of it all—the hundredth of a second caught so precisely that the motion is continued from the picture indefinitely: the moment made eternal." Speed—and its curious connection to things eternal, beyond time. This may be at the center of Crane's work, a reason for both its life and confusion. In "Moment Fugue," the balancing act is tricky and unsettling but absolutely visible.

The poem is built of two stills and a final lunge, its three stanzas quieted by white space via the varied line lengths, the start of those lines flush to the margin, then delayed, then flush and then delayed again, not to mention the small parenthetical dips that suspend what they carry, a kind of thought-bubble, a whisper, a thing barely heard. These stills start in darkness, the flower seller stricken with syphilis but seemingly accepting of his lot at this point, to sell the harmless, beautiful things he sells, the fury of the subway close, vaguely threatening but far away enough. So the poet sets up tension within this first still, two elements at odds, and his authority is established, a bare omniscient sweep right into the head of that flower seller offering violets and daisies, then the fact that he "knows / how hyacinths" . . .

How hyacinths—do, or are, what? In a first, easy read of this piece, one naturally, almost without thinking, drops down into the next stanza, correcting Crane's grammar to realign subject (hyacinths) with verb (offer, not the poet's "offers") and thus fill in what the flower seller must be sure of: "how hyacinths / This April morning offer"—well, something, yes? Whatever the poem might throw out next. Because this small fix works with most everything that follows. But I must trust his actual language here. In fact, this poet does *not* continue the sentence into the second stanza, has *not* chosen the verb form to take those hyacinths anywhere. They're toast now, cut off, that first sentence incomplete, lost to fragment and its breathless effect.

Which is a way to register speed. Here. Now. No, not now—*what was I thinking?* Hold back, start again. And Crane's omniscience? That's pretty much lost, too. We'll never know what the syphilitic knows. He's a locked box. It's a moment of great humility, a backing off that grants dignity to the flower seller—and reveals a grace and vulnerability in the speaker. Nothing to do after hitting such a nerve but start up again in a bright get-on-with-it fashion, apparently with a brand-new sentence though the poet's refusal to add periods makes this, at best, an assumption. Or it's only the fugue's *in stretto* second voice cutting in and over to wipe out—though not quite—that first not-so-certain sentence. Its phrasing half-ghosts everything to come. In the meantime, here on the surface where most of us live, "April morning" graduates from mere time marker to the subject of Crane's focus as a new stanza begins as the flowers are "sorted freshly" to suggest, no, *bestows* / "On every purchaser / (of heaven perhaps)."

Here the sentence does jump stanzas to continue—at least, I think it does. Poised on the edge of all that white space (so wonderfully following an honest-to-god parenthetical "heaven" and that best of all words, "perhaps"), we enter the third and last stanza and there's the great lunge ahead, a violent turn that deeply rattles and estranges. To recap: It's April, and flowers! Thank you! But a dark bursts in: "His eyes— / like crutches hurtled against glass."

*His eyes.* Every buyer—every reader—is hit with them, after the nervous pause of the stanza break. We see him now, the flower seller, a full history and future there. He's sick and furious and doomed, close up, a trick of the zoom lens. After that genteel bestowing and talk of heaven, those violets and daisies and hyacinths to lighten the day, this *just wanting to have a nice dinner party*—all's abruptly ruined. Whatever knowledge the poet began to claim in that first stanza, this is the genuine stuff, a truth intense and riveting and almost unbearable, every bit of it released by the brilliant and terrible simile: eyes equal crutches equal thrown-against-window. We stop, also shattered, rearing back, not caring anymore or knowing now it's absolutely on-target how the syntax is screwed up again, a new sentence slipped in on the back of the previous one, a frantic kind of *in stretto* layering even as those eyes "fall mute" and go "sudden," the flower seller turning diligent, presumably calm again, "dealing change / for lillies," doing his job.

How many worlds in this blink of an eye? And we just witnessed—my god—what? Such steely recognition must be compassion in its purest sense. And of those changes throughout, of voice and key, of press and release—how many camera clicks, the shutter's "hundredth of a second caught so precisely" one after another, over and over again, to see and remember—as Crane added, amazed, in his note to Stieglitz—"even the transition of the mist-mote into the cloud . . ."

And those roses, the final line delivers them, a presence "no flesh can pass." They've grown huge, hardly possible. But the flower seller is safe behind them, out of reach from our pity—we lesser, too-privileged beings.

# INSTEAD INSTEAD /
# ON CIARAN CARSON

Early in 2012 when I was about to leave for Edinburgh, Ciaran Carson got wind of my Fulbright, inviting me to read at the Seamus Heaney Centre in Belfast. Since Northern Ireland is part of the UK and brief city-jumping is allowed, even encouraged within assigned Fulbright regions, off I went, delighted, for a few days' visit.

I mention this to explain why my husband and I were even *in* Belfast at a table of a cozy place for supper, waiting to meet this amazing Irish poet. Certainly Northern Ireland is rich with poets. And was then as well—Heaney, Medbh McGuckian, Sinead Morrissey, Michael Longley, among others. Into that warm and welcoming place (it was winter, after all) walked—more like *lurked toward us*—a man about my age, bent forward in a wrinkled Columbo raincoat, looking quite furtive, and—I have to say it—a shade comic, which only added to my pleasure. It was Ciaran. Who took the seat across from us.

"I am rereading Proust," he blurted out, first thing. "I know everyone is saying that these days, but I really am!" With that, a most strange and lovely conversation began. (I know *lovely* is probably the most overworked glad adjective in the Commonwealth, but cross my heart, this time it proved accurate.)

I only mention *that* because in reading again so many poems for this meditation on Ciaran Carson's work, I'm convinced Proust is key. Or, at least, the *idea* a lot of us have of Proust. That is to say, *memory* is key—locked in that bite of now infamous madeleine, fragrant, soaked in tea, but going way beyond. And how so much of our memory, personal and communal, gets erased violently or out of exhaustion as years pass. Yet how it creeps back, so eternal-seeming, because we're stuck with remembering no matter what, however down to its bits and parts. This poet takes on two of poetry's great subjects: time and knowledge. How this dual gravity is *earned*, as people like to say now—*that* means everything.

From his first book, *The New Estate*, the poem "Soot" keeps haunting. But why?

On the surface it's a simple, credible narrative. An upper-middle-class matron hires a chimney sweep to clean out what might be a dangerous blockage of soot, ash, maybe twigs, rat bones, all kinds of crap up there. The details of this commonplace interaction are laid out carefully: autumn and its dark, the room stripped as a defensive move against what damage this sweep might do, the carpet "rolled back as if for dancing." The caste system is clear (and universal), but this woman's what-to-say awkward chitchat about the weather is ignored. The hardworking sweep will not engage, thank you, and goes straight to it in silence, kneeling, his "yellow cane creaked up / Tentatively." Of course any reference to this medieval but necessary ongoing trade brings back William Blake's innocent but experienced double-whammy take on his own young sweep, surely another kind of haunting that Carson must have hoped for. Good poems are echo chambers, after all.

What fascinates might fall into the "point of view" territory of the fiction writer (so-called third-person limited, yes?), which in turn governs how we readers peep-tom all of this, into our own point of view. We see as she does. The woman *shrouds* the furniture, and grows *shy* as this chimney sweep enters. The whole room abruptly feels suspect and vulnerable, "newly-spacious," even "her footsteps sounding hollow." Sympathy grows for her and yet we feel for him who keeps to the work at hand, apparently peering up the chimney in a rain of soot, then for real asking that she step outside and look. And the repair *is* happening; she sees "the frayed sunflower" up there, "[b]loom triumphantly." She absorbs this fact through image real but imagined via metaphor in open air, she alone on watch while inside he must be still cranking away, equally solitary. A weird sort of symmetry. A success, sort of.

The fact that we know by heart what probably will happen makes it an old story—nothing new here—and in return, she will deliver the payment to "his soiled hand." It's she who notices that his hand is marked by the work, thus we do. And each will go about whatever they must attend to, later in the day. The point is we lose him. It's technically over; narrative ends. But poetry doesn't.

Here's the thing, really two things: *story* is what we remember, *poetry* what we discover. In fact, the room *is* altered in spooky, secret ways. First "a weightless hush / Lingered in the house for days . . ." Fair enough, I guess, though presumably the carpet's unrolled, back as it was, the chairs un-ghosted, everything "spotless" now. But the past is never past, especially in Belfast, beloved city of so many wounds where this poet was born, then lived a life. And it is wounds that make poems.

It's like years later, in Ciaran Carson's brilliant signature book *Belfast Confetti*, in his poem "Turn Again" where

> Someone asks me for directions, and I think again. I turn into
> A side street to try to throw off my shadow, and history is
>     changed.

Because, reading "Soot," the mundane but extraordinary happens: I must turn the page. My own hand lifts the poem into whatever's next, where a final stanza looms. That accidental pause and turn make literal the shift to future time and season, to a new *space* of mind. The woman learns that the soot she swept up will feed the flowerbeds. And in rain, could make its way down

> Sleeping, till in spring it would emerge softly
> As the ink-bruise in the pansy's heart.

There is a curious quiet astonishment here and only a rare, lasting poet, a brave one, would keep going like this straight into transformation. Unlike Carson, many of us—dutiful reporters of the human story—would stop happily enough, going silent when the conventional narrative fades out.

When I think of this poem, everything arrows in and widens and deepens with that *ink-bruise*. The most unprepossessing flower, ordinarily doomed by diminutive cuteness, becomes history and prophecy, warning and solace. The pansy: a startling redefinition of hurt and survival.

Which is an honest-to-god epiphany. I stare down at my hand as if holding that flower there.

# AH

If you move to the mountains, you hope for a decent window. In some states, they tax that—the view, I mean. The *view tax*, it's called. *Don't be viewy*, Ezra Pound insisted—one of his many pushy cautions in "A Few Don'ts," first published in *Poetry* magazine, March 1913—a bit of contemporary-sounding rabble-rousing that might be useful real estate advice in New Hampshire these days, a place which levies such a tax, given the beauty of its landscape. But Pound was only fearing the extraneous *pretty* and *precious* in poems, gratuitous frosting on the cake itself. We greedy eaters forget it is high heat and chemical transformation that really matter—plain flour and sugar, eggs, a little warm milk.

Back to real estate (the *real* estate), just imagine what taxes W. H. Auden would have paid for his evocation of Bruegel's rich landscape in his greatest-hit poem "Musée des Beaux Arts" with its sweep of pond and woods and field that the painter saw or imagined where a ploughman looks down into dirt. There is the sun, and a passing ship and, right out of myth, Icarus, "a boy falling out of the sky" against everyone else's *big deal, so what?*—if it's noticed at all, this "accident" waiting to happen by its crazy ambition and feathers and wings made of wax brought too close to the sun. Through Bruegel's eye, and thanks to Auden, we as readers are positioned in the box seat of *why it matters*, knowing some things turn ironic and still move us à la the big picture: *viewy* and *Oh* at first, then into a gradual and fully fleshed-out *Oh no*.

The soothing take-charge voice that guides us through Auden's poem insists on a premise of what's what and always has been. "About suffering, they were never wrong, / The Old Masters . . ." he tells us calmly, straightaway, which does suggest *get ready for great*, this greatest hit: the believable sound of that over-voice, public and private, large and small at once somehow. Memorable. But what makes a poem great—and lasting? The "quality of its insight," insisted James Tate in an essay once—as in, we're stunned, slowly nodding, drawn in and along for good reason. In any fine piece of writing, a huge silence eats us alive once those carefully chosen words quit coming. Auden's famous final stanza whose few bars many of us can practically hum by heart includes the context for the boy's fall from grace, as depicted in Bruegel's painting of Icarus: how everything "turns away," including the man at his plough though he "may / Have heard the splash, the forsaken cry," or "the white legs disappearing into the green / Water . . ."

In fact this piece unnerves quietly, and in such a push-pull, nonchalant way Auden seems to be saying *for instance*, as if picking up a penny on the sidewalk to examine. It's not so much the legendary and dire consequences for the boy—a foregone conclusion—but the whiplash fact of impending tragedy and everyone's shrugging it off, the human minutiae. Is that terrible, or a relief? In Auden's poem, a waggish touch—something the equally wry Elizabeth Bishop surely loved about his work—is a quality amplified, I think, by the surprise of so many enjambed lines, his complicated but graceful sentences threaded down through them. Against Auden's cool and elegant control, it's also the effect of certain down-home images that quirk up and please—dogs "in some untidy spot" going on "with their doggy life" or the "torturer's horse" idly scratching "its innocent behind on a tree." Such playfulness rides shotgun for a moment, creating a double-take's distance on *oh*, morphing into *oh no*, making it *true*— remember?—and closer to us in spite of Auden's lordly omniscience mostly weighing the piece as both figuratively and literally "viewy," seen from a distance.

If the point is "perspective"—looking across and down with such certainty and only briefly at eye-level—then that classic impulse is built right into the syntax, the poem's apparent "no fragments allowed," none of their hesitation or wonky passion, their jagged start and stop. Complete sentences are at work here, a confident mulled-to-death (consider, consider) declarative "big voice" insists until, I bet, Auden would agree with George Oppen, who wrote in his day-book that "the poem is an instrument of thought, or it is a nuisance." One does risk being the resident know-it-all in the room with such posturing—no, think of it as pure nerve and, as such, a freeing agent that projects expanse and release. It's contagious, as habits of art often are. But it is, finally, our choice. We can drink Auden's Kool-Aid and care a lot, or not give a rat's ass. Auden himself seems to do both. His poem is an argument, complete with the premise and ammunition to prove it. Still, he plays with it.

Question: Is "Musée des Beaux Arts" just an arty, urbane upgrade of Robert Frost's "Out, Out—," in which a boy's hand is severed, a life lost, the blood-letting impossible to stop out there on that desolate farm? No high drama, finally, for Frost's boy either. "And they, since they / Were not the one dead, turned to their affairs." Frost chooses to end his poem with a classic New England reserve—or, it chooses him. But his dark, low-key *suck it up* could be Auden's. Still, something *happens* to us via that hard truth; we're automatically included in their visions, swept off and into, beginning to see that way, perhaps even write that way. We become someone else for a moment. We drop into both poems' inevitable *of course, what did you expect?* Turn left, then right, past the *oh no*. Then, we rise.

I keep thinking about that rise, how vital it is, especially in the midnight swamp of story and mood through which poets tend to pole their boats, some of us lost there forever, never getting to the other side. There isn't always a *get over it* lying in wait, some "I'm better for this" nonsense, some sort of happy ending. Poems aren't exactly moral tales, though Brazilian poet Adelia Prado does close in on that edge with her jumpy, weighted work that often melds opposites: the sacred with the profane, past and present, exclamations against questions against reversals by way of a definite wry streak that utterly charms. Consider the clear-eyed title poem of her first collection available in English, thanks to the fine work of translator and poet Ellen Dore Watson. Prado's "The Alphabet in the Park" seems ironic and casual enough, close to that same kingdom of shrug where Auden and Frost at last find authority and its comfort, except she begins there:

> I know how to write.
> I write letters, shopping lists,
> school compositions about the lovely walk
> to Grandmother's farm which never existed
> because she was poor as Job.

How can anyone stop reading after that? It's witty and endearing. The next few lines turn this initial lie on its head:

> But I write inexplicable things too:
> I want to be happy, that's yellow.
> And I'm not, that's pain.
> Get away from me sadness, stammering bell . . .

The world gets darker and more exact now, however mimed through metaphorical thinking. As if she's speaking to Martians, Prado shorthands our tragic fix. "I live on something called the terrestrial globe, / where we cry more / than the volume of waters called the sea . . ." She cites each river carrying "its batch of tears" but great gladness exists, too, on this planet, and oh boy, "miraculous inventions." Here, her out-of-nowhere fragments and exclamations kick in as she considers the dizzying effect of such a miracle, "a certain Ferris wheel," and wildly digresses, a trademark move for her:

> . . . lights, music, lovers in ecstasy.
> It's terrific! On one side the boys,
> on the other the girls—me, crazy to get married
> and sleep with my husband in our little bedroom
> in an old house with a wood floor.

Then abruptly—characteristically—her wonderful (as in: full of wonder),

> There's no way not to think about death,
> among so much deliciousness, and want to be eternal.

Adelia Prado goes on. Finally, there's this way to end on both hardcore image and spirit drift that, in the grand tradition of poetic closure, actually opens to mystery, to strangeness, to *what?* Joy, that's what, and a lovely savoring alchemy.

> Excuse the expression, but I want to fall in life.
> I want to stay in the park, the singer's voice
> sweetening the afternoon.
> So I write: afternoon. Not the word,
> the thing.

Thus, yet another map to get out of poems alive. In that continuing whirl of "bummer lit," the appeal of *Oh* sliding into *Oh no* can take us farther. Not to happiness exactly. But *step back.* Savor. Take a breath. And—*ah*—it sinks in slowly.

Through the many cubbies and antechambers of poetry as a vast Museum of the Humanly Possible, other shapes and hairpin turns of misfortune and fortune make way for such an exhale—the dark jubilance of Gerald Stern, say, or Walt Whitman, or the underground lifelines of a Carl Phillips, a Larry Levis, a Mary Szybist. Perhaps more to the point, there's Lucia Perillo, who begins her poem "The Second Slaughter" with a little time travel, dipping down into the ancient world to see Achilles slaying and rabid-scary enough for a place in our era— its Middle East where endless bombing continues, where egrets are "covered in tar" from oil well accidents near a marsh, the speaker taken to task by someone for mourning the fate of the wrong species, mere egrets, her worry about the animals first. "So now I guard / my inhumanity like the jackal," she tells us, and further draws out the analogy with gritted teeth to end the poem with a dazzling *human* defiance:

> who appears behind the army base at dusk,
> come there for scraps with his head lowered
> in a posture that looks like appeasement,
> though it is not.

That phrase, *it is not,* in her final line is a sudden steely insistence, doing what closure should: it *opens* to the secret life, a life lived and painfully considered, the complexity of it. Surely, we've passed over from the great *oh no* to *ah!* in spite of cultural and poetic fashions, all the *should*s and *you must*s that keep us back.

In a similar way, Brigit Pegeen Kelly's arguably most beloved poem, "Song," carries a personal secret culled from the great world via an actual news report, as in, yes, this happened: girl with goat, goat done in by unspeakably thuggish boys who thought the whole business funny, a big fat joke. No matter how many times we read this piece, we sicken as the narrative rolls forward by way of Kelly's richly odd, dreamlike telling.

Here's an altered cut-to-the-quick on it, and why we are talking the most serious writing here. Whatever the word "literature" means, it's a huge step above the mere reporting on a tragic story. Which is to say, when that real plot ends, the poem does not. In this case, those guilty boys "would learn to listen," the poet reminds us, past the wind and the "night bird" and their own hearts "beating harder," to hear the ghostly sound that began early in the poem from the goat, the head they took pains to sever and hang high in a tree, now "at last, a song" and "just for them." It's *learn, murmur, remember.* It's *cruel* and *no, not cruel at all.* And, against all expectations, *sweet*, a lost boy haunted by "his mother's call."

That crucial trapdoor secreted away in all great work opens *inward*, from public back to private and in this particular moment, a fierce come-uppance for those boys, sure, but something enormous and brutal is passed on to us, too—all those dark things we carry and will never get rid of, a sweetness that nevertheless cuts the heart. Call it *ah*, another kind of *I get it; isn't this the way of the world?* In certain lights, that's a kind of solace. As in Brigit Kelly's much later poem, "Black Swan," an unfolding from a simple, almost whimsical beginning—"I told the boy I found him under a bush. / What was the harm?"— takes us past the pond and a crumbling sculpture of horses, through "ancient trees" and "things of such beauty" that "I might / Have forgotten, had not the boy . . . Come to me . . . weeping because some older boys / Had taunted him and torn his new coat . . ." It's the boy then, with his furious wish that he'd be "back under the bush." It's that, the poet tells us, which "made the garden rise up again."

All seems struck, stained now, the birds and pond and the cold coming on. Then, finally, this sound in the air, this: "The giant stone hooves of the horses, / Striking and striking the hardening ground." That we remember the garden at all, that it "rises up" and, now, its great shade, too: maybe we knew it all along. Is that a good thing or a bad thing—or, just a thing that keeps deepening? *Ah* is the wiliest creature of all, impossible to pinpoint. Will it open or close?

I want to stay longer at that secret door—the lyric impulse in any poem. It shifts and reveals the *viewy* expanse that we climb a hill and work so hard to see. For what? For something we'd never in a million years expect. News flash: there's no formula or doctrine for this maddening thing that comes to us demanding to be made, no matter where it comes from and how many years or days or split seconds it takes for us to *get it*, damn it, to begin to write it down.

George Oppen scribbled this in his daybook too: "I do not care for systems. What concerns me is the philosophy of the astonished."

Yes.

# SHIRT

One word. But it depends on the word, I suppose.

Chicago, circa 1962, at my parish school, an army of boomer-kids, about fifty of us, shuffled in from lunch and recess to find the word *shit* scribbled on the blackboard in Sister Mary Generose's seventh-grade class. Hastily written, just that word, no exclamation point, not embedded in some snarky phrase for personal assault, zip. It was a pure abstraction. If faced today, not much more than a shrug, an eye roll, or a nod of amused agreement would come of it. But in the early 1960s, that particular word in chalk was the gauntlet thrown down in a battle of dire consequence, a flare in the night sky, an unthinkable instance of outrageous nerve, especially in Catholic school.

Our teacher rushed up to erase it and, threatening Armageddon if we so much as cleared our throats, sped off to confer with her compatriots of wimple and full black habit. What happened next: a spelling test from nowhere and she read aloud what we were to eke out—*chemistry, nasturtium, ridiculous, hieroglyphics*. Next came *shirt*. Just *shirt*, clearly a "baby word," we sneered later, getting the drift: a trap our teachers had set to bring down the culprit with a similar-sounding something that seemed written in a similar hand. (Though who knew, wiped from the board so fast?)

In any case and therefore: rock-bottom proof.

Aha! they must have said and most certainly thought, that small gaggle of nuns riffling pointedly through our tests. See the way he makes his *t*, his *s*? Edward K—! What a surprise, the infamous *bad boy* with his sharp tongue and vast indifference. Also: lock-jawed, steely-eyed, gorgeous, austere, his posture ramrod-straight. And was it really Edward who dashed off that word on the board? I think *yes* then *no*, but most of the time, *who cares*. My husband likes to imagine the oldest nun there as that school rebel, slipped into dementia, loosening the bonds of eighty-nine years of inhibition.

What I remember has narrowed over the years to a glimpse, a flash, a doorway that the Roman god Janus must have guarded with his terrifying doubled face, one side looking back, the other far into the future. It was mythic and thrilling; I sat right by that door. Edward's mother had been called to school. She was weeping in the hallway, ferociously fragile, making sad piercing noises between the two nuns meant to handle this atrocity. And Edward, defiant and beautiful, chin raised, eyes on some amazing lifetime to come stood near her, silently enduring the "case" against him. Expulsion. He was out, his course set. One word can turn the key.

Or, one stray image. Thus a claim I heard once about Joseph Conrad, that on shipboard briefly he'd seen a figure in a deck chair reading, then not reading at all. How the old man held his magazine, the way one leg lay casually over the other, a cigarette between forefinger and thumb, his tweed overcoat neatly folded beneath, etc. And so *Victory*, I was told, Conrad's fourteenth novel, launched itself. True or not, this is exact: just a quick look. The time-stop power of pure attention. One is struck down, pinned, smitten.

What's the standard phrase? *I'll never, ever forget* . . . In my case, so many ghostly bits hang on but among them that poor woman in collapse, the officious nuns panicked by a silly nick of profanity, the brilliant resistance in a boy framed and already sure that out there a world waited. Then, he was gone.

As for *Victory*, it became a part-time job to help keep us afloat. In my twenties, I read the novel *to* someone, a sizable section each day for the ancient woman who'd hired us to cook for her too, in the downstairs apartment of the old house my husband and I shared with her. He and I took turns with the reading, quietly absorbing each other's chapters on our off-days, to keep up.

I walked downstairs to another world. But I distinctly remember hearing Conrad in my own voice, mouthing *his* words, though I didn't find—at least can't recall now from those pages—the man who smoked and stared out to sea, who unknowingly burrowed into that writer so deep that a whole book, a rich inner life to continue and cherish, came of it.

# "BENT AS I WAS, INTENTLY"

Just to be clear: I love Charles Simic's poems; they turn and rewind, then: *look!* And how skewed but *normal* his stuff seems, fated and hopeless and ancient and new. It's a spell of sorts and that's *joy*, his surprise, his quirky imbalance, such grounded weirdness in it. I'm writing this off the top of my head, which I fear opens not like a sturdy envelope but an old Pez dispenser, a sweet, if minor, offering because it's late May, the northern hemisphere overwhelmed with the season's standard amazement: trees sudden into leaf, flowers knowing exactly what to do with blue and red and yellow. Yay, you fiddlehead ferns! Uncurl thyselves to sky and rain.

As for Simic, I discovered him in 1968 when I sprang for Paul Carroll's anthology, *The Young American Poets*. I'm not even sure Simic had published a collection yet. (Since then, I've picked up a second copy at a garage sale, jubilant but disbelieving: How could anyone let go of that marvelous book to sell in a driveway next to the old Mix Master and a cardboard box of Tupperware?) In any case, and in that earlier fit of luck, I discovered Simic's work. And keep finding it, over and over, grateful again. That's what it is to be in the good company of such a stranger. You forget, then abruptly remember.

It makes sense to think through one poem. I've been rereading rather desperately for days, rattling each collection like a box, as if a single dazzlement might fall out, a perfect tooth left behind by the fairy. A sign.

I thought I wasn't asking much. But outside, the spring ferns too are hard to figure. I understand they grow, yet they appear to be a series of stills overall, mysteriously altered each morning, ferns to unwind and straighten as days pass deeper. Not exactly a flip book, but how on earth did this happen? If I picked one, if I dragged out my little field box of watercolors to nab one on paper . . .

All these terrific poems of Charles Simic for decades: How to do that walkabout with only one? I mean, there's "Brooms," always lying in wait for me inside that book with one of the world's great titles, *Return to a Place Lit by a Glass of Milk*—

> Only brooms
> Know the devil
> Still exists,
>
> That the snow grows whiter
> After a crow has flown over it . . .

Simic goes on, any broom "a tree / In the orchard of the poor" or a "roach there . . . / a mute dove."

This is only the first section, and the poem comes early in his life's work, but every bit of Simic is here: his way with personification (how does he do this, minus sentimentality?), his more and more high-contrast, fabled detail—that crow against snow, those corners where we all want to dream off. Here, that broom, a tree, a *roach* as deliberate and passionately needed as a dove. Public and private. World within world within world, always at an angle. Nothing's merely whatever it is. The dove all by itself gets strange too—its well-known song "mute," but emphatic single stresses underscore, open, still the heart. This poet hears things, regardless.

Forgive me. I'm way overboard. But this is *Simic*, for god's sake. Young poets have heroes. He was definitely one of mine forty years ago. And still. But back there in my own stone age, he was one reason I started to write poems at all.

Another favorite. From his third book, *Dismantling the Silence*, the poem "To All Hog-Raisers, My Ancestors," which is wry and serious, crazy-moving somehow, and I like to imagine it speaks to half of my gene pool, those wily Eastern Europeans who got here cheap, in steerage, or never left the Old Country. On and on about their "solemn business" of eating pork, the sense of "land they worked on." (Note: "worked on," never "owned.") Then, from a listserv so familiar (plus honest, plus unnerving), those "Turnip-headed drunks, horse-thieves, / Lechers, brutes, filthy laborers . . ." back there in the muddy human seed bank. Welcome to the most unsettling family reunion ever. Welcome to Simic: the oddest uptick of ambition, plus more trademarks—shady, matter-of-fact, hilarious.

> If I add garlic to my pork
> It is for one who became a minister . . .
> Changed his name, never to be heard of again.

But I will run a single poem through the X-ray machine for ghostly halos and shadow in spite of whatever seeming clarity and streetwise charms mark this piece. Thus, "Whispers in the Next Room" from *Classic Ballroom Dances* takes on the hospital barber, what he does without favor, across the board, what this widower eats alone in his flat, his curious, heartbreaking-as-usual prayer.

First, the title, those "whispers" we lean toward and simply *overhear*—which is one of Auden's claims about poems that I've always loved and keep bringing up until people want to gag me. The word itself "whispers" with a stifled S twice to damp-down the who or how many are speaking that low. The backdrop complicates with ". . . the *Next* Room" (my italics). Given the whispering—an exchange? a conversation?—is it really only the ghost of future or past, a wisp of cloud or smoke? Frost too is here, his valuable notion about tracking "sentence sounds" and his thoughts about poet as listener behind a door, or in the same room, eavesdropping on the end of a phone call with its pause and pause, its wind-down, a kind of music broken for both ear and page. Simic, so regularly smitten with a declarative syntax and his stubborn-paced, stately, out-of-fashion quatrains, seems keyed from the get-go to a measured sound, often on repeat. Certainly there's more of poetry's history in such spatial and formal distancing—"The women come and go, speaking of. . . ." Well, you-know-who, and who famously keeps telling us that. With

Simic's speaker, as with Eliot's, we are positioned in some eternal time zone, alert, head to the side, absorbing everything. All bets are off in this piece that enacts the mystery of origin and the self.

As with his "turnip-headed drunks," Simic uses character here to tap what feels an old story that makes for a quirky empathy. He writes tiny fables, book after book populated with vignettes and figures as odd as they are familiar, at times unsavory. This protagonist, though, I looked him up: barbers have been shaving people since at least 3000 B.C.E. Think the natty ancient Egyptians at the very least, hair on every part of the body cut close as if they could slippery-slip back one day into the womb toward a glorious afterlife. Way before that, with sharpened clamshells under some stony overhang, those almost-human in their Neanderthal slump were apparently shaving something too. This poet begins quite specifically:

> The hospital barber, for instance,
> Who shaves the stroke victims,
> Shaves lunatics in strait-jackets . . .

Picture it. Hardcore image as vigil light, as horrifically commonplace. That's Simic, his eye dark and brief, the layering built with casual care. Taking his time, the poet gives us more on this barber until we have what fiction writers like to say is a "narrative arc" and to which poets say, "okay, a progression, I give you that." We strain to hear, curious about this figure who comes to us first as a mere "instance," somehow arriving midstream, as proof of something. But of what?

Soon enough his backstory kicks in via shorthand notes or a list of statements that never quite end (instead those breathless, savoring, shrugging ellipses), cast in lines with the subject largely implied, silently carried over, but less and less an afterthought—*for instance* added to the title. He emerges as the main presence "who shaves" all the long day then returns home to supper to make one long dangling sentence of the poem, engineered to keep going by pause and hesitation. This barber,

> Is a widower, has a dog waiting
> At home, a canary from a dimestore . . .

A dime store! Cherished site of childhood drama and being. The word opens up a semi-sacred place where "helmeted divers plummet," as Laura Jensen wrote once about the back wall of murky tanks and shining fish some of us might recall, then drift off in the remembering.

I digress. But poems call across world and time to each other, exactly what should happen via their separate dream and parallel orbits . . . And Simic's canary! I'd argue it is genius to recover that creature, to suggest a small, gold-singing insistence that could drive you nuts.

Meanwhile, the poem's ordinary steadfast barber, home now, is down to supper, his canned beans cold, going for the bottom "with a spoon."

Hear it? The whispering might well include the slow and meticulous drag of the metal every hand and hunger know well. The get-it-all, every bite, is desire, a minimum elegant gratitude for what little this world offers. The vanishing ellipses in both cases mean *please, never cease, O dime store, O spoon . . .* We witness this fellow at work, at home, but it's these plainsong side notes, simple images that nail poignancy, the disturbing and dearest bits. (*Connect, connect* says the poem, forever echoing Forster, bringing his well-loved dictum-unto-cliché to new life.)

They hover in the wings, the damaged one in his strait-jacket, the stroke victim still hanging around, another neuro-lightning bolt threatening any second, both men unable to see what they've come to, no mirror, no way. Because the barber isn't completely sealed and silent. He speaks the last stanza to—to us? To himself? To the dead? The disguise is prayer, meaning loss and invocation and ache as he claims invisibility: "No one has seen me today" and "Oh Lord, as I too have seen / No one, not even myself . . ."

We also lean and hover, exactly as that barber did—"Bent as I was, intently, over the razor"—what he was paid to do. It's Simic again, keeping everything *as is* by the unsaid but suggested, the darkest dark going inward to lodge there.

Close is far; to look up is key. First and finally, what do we know of anything? Maybe poems at heart are moral tales, thus a reduction. I hope not. But we disappear in them to find out something, and at times live there for days.

# IN THE DREAMTIME

Most days, in what seems to me now the huge middle of my life, I woke at about 4 A.M. to stare at the blank page and write poems. I savored the quiet house, everyone else sleeping. And often part of that spiritual discipline, even before I began to write, meant reading a poem by Laura Jensen.

It hardly mattered which one, each a deep disconnect in spite of its dailiness, its skewed clear-eyed look into a common world—dime stores, jets overhead, bus stops, hanging up laundry in the yard. I was profoundly here but somewhere else. In an interview long ago in the *Northwest Review*, Jensen told Greg Simon that "my poetry is very much 'if' and 'possibly.'" As for me, I hear an *on-the-verge-of* in Jensen's remark, each poem a door, a secret entrance. I can pretend now a pre-dawn and that I am on that verge again, an *almost*, about to listen for, absorb, work on whatever will fall to me: an image, a shard from my own life. But first, to clear the electrocardiogram, to be empty enough.

Say I am reading "Calling," one of my favorite poems of Jensen's. Here is its fourth stanza:

Come down, come down and stop your dreaming.
The house grew old as I grew old
and has turned into a waiting.

Remote. Stopped. Just the feel of that: maybe I *can* cross over somehow, calm down and open for good or ill, to my own odd whatever-will-come.

For years I have told my students that mystery is not confusion. I've told them a lot of things, mostly forgettable even to me. But this primal exactitude about writing poems is not. And Jensen taps right into it, unafraid but aware. Poems require a bit of fear too, a profound unsettling. To be of the world but not of this world—that's Jensen. I'm not sure where that strange expanse in the imagination might be, or begin to be, but when any of us are writing well, we are its original unruly citizens.

Once I was lucky to be in an extended conversation with Laura Jensen. There were a few of us asking her various questions about her practice or the poems themselves. The whole business was strange. She would suddenly say something confounding, a non sequitur of sorts. I'd been trying to think it through, jump the synapse with her. Then I realized it wasn't a leap at all. Under the ongoing run of our talking, part of her was still back there, mulling over an earlier question, and finally ready at this later point to address it. And there was her answer, abruptly before us.

There is something of that layering in her poems, a way of collecting experience and idea, holding it back in parts, in quietude, until it returns, as if on its own—a drifting, however altered by the press of such reverie. Past wandering underneath, and into the present and beyond. That is no small thing. And it's not patience exactly. It's a matter of *origin*.

In 2019, I spent five months in Australia on a Fulbright. One of the many things that continues to fascinate is the Indigenous concept of "Dreamtime"—"in the Dreamtime," a phrase said quite a bit and meaning many things, some of them private, never to be available to the uninitiated, such as the likes of me. But from what I can understand, these are often stories of origin, ways to see what's called *Country* (note: not "the" country), and the human *ongoingness* with it; up to seventy thousand years in Australia. The default a kind of layering, where now *was*, where future circles back.

When I consider the little I can grasp of the Dreamtime against the vast expanse of the outback I've seen, it's not a stretch at all, that deep nothing brought on by one of Jensen's poems before I began to work my own out of the darkest morning those years ago. And tomorrow, if I'm lucky.

No way to explain further, which might be exactly the point. Wallace Stevens was right: thought does collect in pools. But it isn't a pool. It's probably not even thought.

# UNLIMITED

Carl Sandburg is not high on the literary food chain these days, but when I was a teenager and falling in love with poems, I was all over his work. He was still alive, though an old man. We were both from Illinois, and my much-loved, *old* grandparents in whose downstate house I spent a lot of my summers equaled, in my mind, the world Sandburg wrote of—prairie and cornfields, a single-street downtown, a county courthouse with its Civil War cannon rusting out front. In short, the Midwest, *not* a place I ever saw in everything else I was reading, really inhaling: dumb novels and smart ones, other poems, the backs of cereal boxes, breathless or matter-of-fact notes and shopping lists left behind on the pavement by strangers.

Sandburg's first book, his *Chicago Poems*, was a favorite, many of its pieces initially published in *Poetry* magazine. I'm still amused and thrilled when I think of his biographical notes in those early issues, things like *Carl Sandburg is a bricklayer in Chicago.* "Look under something," my mother always advised, though that was usually aimed at lost keys. Here is Sandburg's 1916 poem, "Limited"—

> I am riding on a limited express, one of the crack trains of the
>     nation.
> Hurtling across the prairie into blue haze and dark air go
>     fifteen all-steel coaches
> holding a thousand people.

(All the coaches shall be scrap and rust and all the men and
    women laughing
in the diners and sleepers shall pass to ashes.)
I ask a man in the smoker where he is going and he answers:
    "Omaha."

Why this poem in his first book was the kicker for me, I'm not
sure; it does befit classic teen angst, the *what-do-you-shallow-grown-
ups-know-about-life?* attitude of that age group. I imagine "Limited"
set down certain angles of vision toward poetry itself for me: that
there are two worlds, seen and unseen; what's right now but how time
will alter that; the cheap bangles over what's genuine (my mother's
*look under something*, abruptly widened).

There were more technical gifts, too. You *can* use the immediate
present tense to keep this going forever. Plus ordinary details can be
crucial *and* poignant. A solid first-person speaker lives in, and guides,
Sandburg's poem, which is both contained and expansive in its imagery, those steely trains so wisely made to cross a continent of grassland
and farms and woods and cities and poverty and fortune. There's
thinking—via assertion and the underground parenthetical—and
conversation, a sense of myth and miraculous in the ordinary, rust
and ashes waiting in what is snappy-fast and gleaming. Nothing is
as it seems. Anyway, poems can't just lollygag around, being sen-
sitive and emoting (at sixteen, I was already good at both). At the
least, they can get dramatic: something happens in, and to, the world
within them.

Quite a bit of *doing* for a mere six lines! Of course, loved by adolescents and grown-ups alike, irony lives in every word, especially the
last one, *Omaha*—admittedly overwrought, lowered like the proverbial boom, a punchline though the heavy-ominous, the not-funny. I
showed the poem to my friends in high school. Sandburg was *the man*.

Although he worked all manner of jobs—as a social reformer,
as a journalist whose coverage of the Chicago Race Riot of 1919
was honored by the NAACP, as an award-winning biographer of
Lincoln—now, in spite of his two Pulitzer Prizes in poetry, we think
of his poems as somewhat squishy, overly romantic, his ambition
toward the epic and the American dream a lame knock-off of Whitman and his open arms, a poet of another age.

But I keep a postcard of Sandburg pinned to our kitchen bulletin board, a wonderful shot of the young poet and his wife, Lilian, taken by her brother, the revered early twentieth-century photographer Edward Steichen, and given to me by my brother. I like to look at it, now and then. I like to be reminded.

# MIDDLE KINGDOM

Think *Midwest*, I tell myself. And—to be honest—at first I think not much at all. That's a great thing. What a generous, unobtrusive landscape! Or, I think *map*, but past that infamous *New Yorker* cover—East Coast, West Coast, and the vast blank flyover to ignore or endure in the middle. Because those unwieldy paper maps we actually used for years (and some still use) weirdly resemble the actual feel of the place. In a kind of comforting matter-of-fact awe, you unfold them as best you can, lay them out landmass-flat on the passenger seat of the car, follow your forefinger along county lines and little starred towns broken and linked somehow by a distance of wind and rain, roadkill and telephone pole after telephone pole.

The song of the field sparrow might be the perfect soundtrack to this—plain, mesmerizing, horizontal-strange, and somehow comforting. It's described exactly in the bird books: "an accelerating whistle that ends in a trill, a rhythmic pattern similar to that of a ping-pong ball dropping on a table." But mostly, birdsong aside, it occurs to me now that this expanse, this silence of the Midwest, is also a mindset, a way of thinking about human existence, *being* itself, a primal *before* and an eerie *after*. It may be, at heart, an oxymoron to ramble on, this *talking* about maps that mime such quiet. What it amounts to: *Stop. Lay down your weapons. Shut up; look harder.*

Of course, there are larger shapes, region to country to continent, maps mainly an abstract notion of the real thing, prone to imagination's flight. I think of my childhood state, Illinois—shaped, I thought as a kid, like a lucky rabbit's foot, though, admittedly, I see now that the rabbit is not so lucky. Or how Lake Michigan ballooned out and down, and my native city, Chicago, was just a little dot at its lower left. Or the great sweep of water where the world began beyond Lake Shore Drive, the smartest urban thinkers in history deciding to leave it plain grass and sand, not build those blocky skyscrapers right up to edge of blue unto blue. Amazing! *They did not murder the view.* Carl Sandburg has a poem, "The Harbor," that got it right:

> I came sudden, at the city's edge,
> On a blue burst of lake,
> Long lake waves breaking under the sun
> On a spray-flung curve of shore;
> And a fluttering storm of gulls,
> Masses of great gray wings
> And flying white bellies
> Veering and wheeling free in the open.

Sure, it could be that only a landlocked flatlander from Galesburg, Illinois—as Sandburg was—could truly thrill to such a moment. But I think it's contagious.

Meanwhile, so many fine writers were born Midwesterners but moved east or west—Theodore Dreiser, Hart Crane, Langston Hughes, F. Scott Fitzgerald, Mark Twain, Marianne Moore, Theodore Roethke, Kurt Vonnegut—and as far off as London, where T. S. Eliot ended up, the guy promptly acquiring a British accent as camouflage. Though Gwendolyn Brooks stayed in Chicago, Sandburg himself eventually packed up and moved to North Carolina with a small band of noisy, irascible goats. There's never seemed to be a clear regional *voice* or close identification with the Midwest like the South's pull on the most edgy and enduring Flannery O'Connor, Eudora Welty, Carson McCullers, or its myth-rendering William Faulkner. Certainly, the Midwest has never been like the self-congratulatory East, its historical *first-here-and-forever* weight such a burden on new writers. Or—in reverse—the *blow-it-off-don't-look-back* (yahoo!) of the West.

Instead, Midwesterners got the ache, the doubt—too many doubts—the shadow, the shrug, the wisecrack, a feel for hope and desperation in equal amounts. Those of us of this Middle Kingdom, fled or unfled, apologize without reason because we're prophets or maybe we're bored, or because we really are sorry about everything and haven't a clue what to say. Or because we're curious, and then obsessed, always a new trapdoor to yet another cellar of pain or remorse. We're never that far from the dark.

Specific things I cherish from my childhood in the Midwest: reading Robert Bly and James Wright for the first time forty years ago, and Sandburg, for that matter, and seeing on the page what I loved in my grandparents' small down-state town: cornfields continually ticking off the long drives, weedy brick sidewalks to be walked, old houses with porches where people actually sat and held forth about neighbors or the world, whichever came first. "Suddenly a small bridge," Bly wrote, ". . . a few people are talking low in a boat," or his "old men sitting on car seats" in some beloved trashy front yard. Astonishing—and familiar. That one could write about honest-to-god actual things!—and, as the Kansas City–born poet James Tate blurted out in an essay: *not* have to be August Swinburne after all. Like my own *What a relief!* I've never stopped recalling my favorite moment in *Huckleberry Finn*, where, holed up on an island in the Mississippi, Huck turns to Jim and says in utter pleasure: *I wouldn't want to be nowhere else but here.* Then this, about writing poems or stories—and perhaps the oddest flash of all: that things *become* real, mysterious, and wildly layered *as you write about them.* Thus, you live there.

Though Allen Ginsberg discounted his own claim *first thought, best thought,* surely it's initially *place, place, place* where a writer really begins, meaning: *begins to see.* It's not exactly like my serious gratitude that my mother was a terrible cook, which has made every meal put before me since into something to cheer and relish. But I am glad that the beauty I saw first—no rapturous mountains or glorious ocean-blue waves—didn't stun breathlessly, inarguable, no further thought required. In the Midwest, beauty was small, quirky, confusing, framed by a window, the edge of a table, a hand that pointed the way somewhere.

Living in—or being from—the Midwest is not really a calling, nothing that befits a T-shirt printed to extol such a claim or confession. But it *is* a discipline. One has to stare longer, to be stranger. Here, drink this, says the region's particular, peculiar muse.

So that's a kind of overture, I suppose. Any small expanse might enlarge an initial blurt to further exploration, even this one, about the *Middle Kingdom*, a term, by the way, coined by the ancient Chinese, a kind of proud selfie.

Back to the Midwest, there's a more relevant point of historical interest, more humbling and vulnerable: the place once pulverized, ground down into a seeming nothing, leveled by a glacier twelve thousand years back, that seemingly unending dump of ice a mile high, I've been told. Think of all the dirt and stone and ice scraping along loudly, once dragged beneath where Midwesterners sit and stand and dream at night. A monster, a literal force of nature and, in its wake, a near-oceanic expanse, a legacy. It *is* like the Great Nothing that New Yorkers or Californians notice, looking down from their oxygen-thinning heights.

The thing is, I love this about the Middle Kingdom, that it is literally *the middle of a continent.* I love that it not only bores those flyover sorts, those East or West Coasters—that it scares them. One can drive between towns and see everything as if knocked back and long gone, a route to some afterlife, a kind of visual hush to the horizon, the very definition of *distance.* You might go inside yourself to see it mirrored there, where it *is* unsettling, how an impending storm slowly gets closer, clouds of the darkest dark, wind solid and steady, nothing to stop it. A Midwestern given: geography as pure elegy, one of absence and loss and premonition, what writer Michael Martone has comically—I'd say poignantly—dubbed *the flatness*, however painfully acquired by glacier and grit.

There is another complication, thanks to that massive sheet of ice, one laid out brilliantly in a very curious book, *Reading the Landscape* by May Watts, first published in 1957 and going into ten editions. A lively chapter explores one of the Midwest's sacred spots—Indiana's Turkey Run State Park, where, grinding its way south, that ancient glacier carried bits from a mysterious elsewhere that took root in the upper slopes of its trails, its trees and shrubs and ferns and flowers so drastically out of place, dragged down from the "green tooled-leather forest floor of northern Wisconsin, or northern Michigan, or Maine." Watts meant partridgeberry and winterberry, the yew and the hemlock, this "little band of northerners, acquainted with the song of the hermit thrush" (the state bird of Vermont, after all) "clinging"—she tells us, "to the cliff's edge." The Midwest as a "big table" welcoming all— one of legendary Chicago poet Paul Carroll's favorite expressions for a series, Big Table was a sort of Midwestern Yale Series of Younger Poets that he envisioned before his publisher, Follett, changed course and dropped it after four wonderful debut collections by Bill Knott, Dennis Schmitz, Andrei Codrescu, and Kathleen Norris.

What came next in the geo-history of the region is worth greater detail. Enormous forests sprang from those well-traveled seeds and bits, near two millennia's worth. A tireless, leafy intervention for centuries, trees (maple, hawthorn, sycamore, oak) filled up that glacier-pitched, rich, watery rock-bottom—trees everywhere eventually, a lush *once-was* before white settlement gradually stripped it down again. That astonishing forested trace still exists in our memory theaters like dark floaters in the eye. Get out the Ouija board and ask any early settler about it. Or the Indigenous tribal people—the Miami, the Shawnee, and others—here since human time began on the continent. Those great forested expanses hang around, available to the imagination of anyone quiet enough in what woods that have lasted or gone into second, third growth. OMG, trees! Once-massive tracts of them, pre-nineteenth century, high roosts the doomed passage pigeons loved in their great darkening migrations overhead, hours at a time. Garrison Keillor, once doing his *Prairie Home Companion* at Purdue University in 2012, opened his broadcast with the Indiana state song, praising its lyrics with considerable relish: "You really have to love a tune with that much vegetation in it."

The fact is, there are writers raised in the Midwest still haunted by this history. Will Dunlap, for one, in "The Salvation of Doctor MacLeod," his unpublished novel about Indiana life two centuries ago, dreams such a place through his narrator, August MacLeod, a young doctor recalling his childhood:

To think of the countryside as those old men described it, mile upon square mile intensely forested—giant red oaks, sycamores, and tulip poplars so densely clustered in places, their branches so thickly interwoven that only occasionally did sunlight pierce through to the ground. Back then the new-cut road came to little more than a narrow stump-filled track. You might ride dozens of miles before you reached a clearing, before a furl of smoke, that most reliable signal of a claim over nature, caught your eye.

Take that, you disdainful, distracted New Yorkers flying over us, glancing down through your tiny windows from the heaven of complimentary peanuts and Diet Cokes.

It seems right to invite one of the beloved dead into this—another Midwestern habit—and invoke that wily St. Louis native, Marianne Moore, then do a bit of temporary surgery on her poem "A Grave," which I've loved for years. Though on the surface a piece about the ocean, think for a moment: *not exactly*. "Man looking into the sea," she begins for real,

> taking the view from those who have as much right to it as you
>     have to yourself,
> it is human nature to stand in the middle of a thing . . .

Moore keeps at it, bringing forward firs "in a procession, each with an emerald turkey-foot at the top" or birds and their "cat-calls," or the oars of boats "moving together like the feet of water-spiders." So quick and grounded, all of it, so matter of fact her lighthouses and bell-buoys. It's Moore's classic sharp eye for natural detail in this remarkable poem that melds the abstract and the concrete with such quirk and grace.

Consider for a moment a turn on this, a translation of sorts—forgive me, Miss Moore!—into America's own middle kingdom. Instead, what if it were:

> Men looking into *field* unto *field* . . .
> it is human nature to stand in the middle of a thing . . .

Later, in the actual poem, "men lower nets, unconscious of the fact that they are desecrating a grave . . ." If we switch that, shade it landlocked *Midwestern* for a moment as in "men lower *blades and harrows,* unconscious of the fact that they are desecrating a grave," we'd be close to the truth of another small violence repeated on earth endlessly enough.

But what about Moore's claim that it is "human nature to stand in the middle of the thing"? In the middle of the long afternoon and its hunger? In the middle of a life, its glad discoveries or disappointments, or in any really fine poem, the moment deepens through the greatest hesitation of all via unspoken questions: What's really at stake here? Why even bother? And aren't Midwesterners mostly polite, usually second-guessing themselves? To live in the *interior,* in the middle of—pause—whatever it is. Uncertainty? A perpetual unknowing? A forever *turn left, then right, then left again, then*—

Call it thoughtfulness, this *what if* about poems and stories, this *whether* and *oh no* and *well, okay, okay* on a loop, a loop, a loop. Or like the sign I noticed recently in Lafayette, Indiana, tacked up on a pole: *It's okay to change your mind.* Perhaps that's it, *flexible* being a good thing, not completely a *my bad, my bad.* I was stopped at a light, so had time to consider.

To repeat: *It is human nature to stand in the middle of a thing.* If I were the tattooing sort, I'd have my caption right there, worth needle-pointing my arm for, to carry to the end of time—or at least, a mere lifespan—until there is no middle, nothing before and nothing after, just that stab of immediate seeing and feeling, that sense of things *in the center.* All of us are born smack in the middle of whatever intricate, puzzling narrative, large or small, public or private. That's where experience and education come in, our trying to figure how we fit into the world's story, not to mention our own. It *is* human nature to stand *in the middle of a thing,* that uneasy spot where all serious decisions take place: Do I love you, or not? Should we go, or should we stay? When does memory kick in, joy or nightmare replayed enough to haunt and keep us awake at night? When did that first poem or story come to you?

And longing: Is it caught and triggered by an image, a stray word, some terrible realization? I think of that vast glacier again, randomly dragging along seeds from the frozen north, from the past: hemlock and winterberry, forms of life completely out of place where they were dropped but thriving nevertheless, given the impossibly ancient galoot of solid ice that once passed over the landscape, doing damage and bringing its gifts. "The sea is a collector," Marianne Moore says in her poem. So, too, the acres and acres of land keep a rich, legendary hoard intact, either side of Midwestern interstates, the long drive to get from *here* to wherever *there* might be. Beware: you can so easily drift off behind that wheel. Wake up!

It's the *flatness* again. The geography that writers from the Middle Kingdom have been given, literally and as metaphor, is a mindscape, a point of view, a boredom *and* a solace, a thing to flee and embrace, to leave alone or to fill. Either way, region *marks*. Robert Frost famously said we pick up knowledge—or what passes for it—the way anyone walks through pasture, burrs sticking to a pantleg. Praise to these burrs, then, an endless supply of image and second thoughts. They link and repeat and go straight into poems and stories just as fields dizzy up, seem enormous, keep repeating their mystery of corn and corn, their big bluestem and clover. Always in the middle of the thing. Which so often means: stop, look further. Then, start again, in earnest.

A landscape painter might tell us three ways to see, at least three ways to record and recover *what* we see. You can run it into the farthest reach, where sky rises off land, straight into the dream of the lyric. You can shore up and focus on the closest narrative bits, the obvious minutiae one finds first, and immediate—the beloved or the awful, cause before effect. But a truly interesting swath, the most complex and solacing and potentially disturbing, I think, is the *middle distance*, the go-between and in-between, the space on canvas full up or scattered with houses and yards, tiny oxen pulling plows, ordinary human enterprise, the kind Bruegel set up as backdrop and foil to his Icarus flying straight into myth and sun, his wax wings to melt, until he fails gloriously. Bruegel's recounting *is* glorious! The middle distance—where that boy-god *will* fall—where we live out the most crucial parts of the story.

And what does it mean to be a writer from the Midwest? Perhaps all writers, at heart, come from there by way of their aloneness and subversion and restlessness. Some painterly advice I found on the web: you *lighten* for distance; you *darken* what's central. I remember when learning to drive—late, in my thirties—our neighbor in Maine who was teaching me insisted I keep my eyes not on the immediate road looming up, too close but not too far ahead either, certainly not to the horizon line. Keep your eyes up, she said. She meant, keep your eyes on the world—a couple of cars' worth, and either side, a *middle* distance. Middle equals *safe*. That would do the trick. I'd be fearless enough that way, but lurching forward toward home and that most miraculous state of being of all: supper.

"It's human nature to stand in the middle of a thing," Marianne Moore wrote in her poem, ". . . but you cannot stand in the middle of this," she added. Really? Start again in that brave dark, in stillness, in silence. Take your time.

In certain portraits where you have several figures turned to the right or left, it's the woman staring directly at us—into a *middle distance*—who stops us cold. Her blank eye to our blank stare.

It's chilling. An eternity there. I remember that woman. Her gaze is a little off. She's not, in fact, looking at us, is she? She sees herself in us. She sees a human fate.

# COMPUTER BLURS, BLACKOUTS, AUDIO HICCUPS, AND STARDUST

It's a time warp for me at the computer these days. Whether the wheel is inventing me, or me, the wheel, I have no idea. Maybe I just have more trouble with Zoom than other people do. That is, until I talk to some of those people.

The raw alarming fact in a pandemic: shared moments of need stagger us now. The most urgent demands for safety and health pile up. Millions sick, so many in the death count, beyond comprehension. In the presence of this, it feels callow, cheap even, to bring up my complaint. But when I try to see a poetry reading via Zoom, often engineered by a hardworking bookstore owner in a fabulous distant city, it turns out too often a disappointment—though rarely because of the poets or what they've written. Instead, the fits and starts, the semi-failures, lie in the not-so-magical transition through satellite or stardust or whatever conduit's at work. Sudden camera blurs, blackouts, audio hiccups, silences. Still. it *is* something, isn't it, that we can summon up those squares on the screen with faces in them, given this little online *engine-that-can't-quite.*

When Seamus Heaney took the podium in Stockholm to deliver his brilliant Nobel Prize address in 1995, what I did not expect was a pneumatic tube of time travel. Straightaway, all got sucked backwards, fast but detailed enough to be savored. Memory slowed it down. Childhood slowed it down. "I would climb up on an arm of our big sofa to get my ear closer to the wireless speaker," Heaney said.

I *can* see it: an old radio transmitting horrific, dire news of the Second World War. I imagine the sound scratchy unto almost-not, and that faraway boy in Derry straining to figure out the BBC announcer's great world out there, ominous and beyond belief. I use that term "great world" a lot because we do ache for its past and future, especially now that so much is out of reach, coming at us huge but in fragments, stabs of knowing and unknowing, as it came to the boy who would become a justly revered poet.

Updated but not transformed, it is still with us, that long ago beaming *in* by way of an "aerial wire attached to . . . the chestnut tree . . . in through a hole bored in the corner of the kitchen window . . . into the innards of our wireless set where a little pandemonium of burbles and squeaks would suddenly give way . . ." I love the mystery involved, so transferable and personal, those "innards" of the radio, its "little pandemonium" especially. Maybe everything is metaphor.

What we have in common with that boy—a thought that hit as I leaned toward my computer's screen and struggled with Zoom, as my link blinked out then on, and the poets I wanted to hear froze and vanished, finally to get patched in again—is this: time does warp and in doing so, reveals. A boy turns into a man turns into a boy. All of it is ancient, a text.

Is the computer a machine? I'm no longer aware of that.

# THE GREAT SILENCE

⌐

### *Day One*

It's not a story. Meaning: of course I get lost en route. Nothing to do but phone from my car, on the outskirts of a city four hours from my house, semi-hopeless. Not that far, the monk at the other end says. *Take a left, a right, then another left.* Between those turns three long roads and a slow, falling dark.

After an hour, past supper, I arrive, bedraggled. There's a small cemetery to walk through, broken tooth after broken tooth of grave-stones in the shadows on either side. The lost beloveds of nearly two centuries, and others—I suspect a few were perhaps disliked, but they endured and now are honored anyway by their burial here. I spot the wooden double door, the letters cut in granite over it: *PAX*. An email had alerted me: a parking lot, a cemetery, that lovely Latin word in stone.

So I find it, finally, the Abbey of Gethsemani in Kentucky, fifty miles or so southeast of Louisville, the first monastery established in America, 1848, on the frontier's darkest dark among woods, though now it's pastures, fields, and walking trails through what's left of that virgin forest. This is where writer and *here-comes-everybody* thinker Thomas Merton entered the Trappist Order and lived, for years. That he's the point of so many pilgrimages—would that trouble, amuse, or please him? Maybe none of the above.

You got here quick, the monk at reception tells me, he who talked me in as if I were a befuddled pilot barely in control of some rattletrap plane and clueless about landing. Well . . . But *quick*? I look at him in disbelief. In a stroke of kindness, they've held supper for me and I gratefully eat in a corner, a quiet figure over a tray. I will learn this— you always eat alone in this dining room. And it's never *not* quiet. The sign on the wall: *Silence spoken here.*

It's just that words are stones and one by one you put them down. For a week, you don't pick them up.

### Day Two

Before breakfast, I discover the library. Two restored chant books on display, re-bound expertly by a monk, photographs to the side showing the meticulous step-by-step restoration. Each prized page is huge, measuring three hands high. *Ad Vigilias*, this chant is called. Its small, linked black squares indicate notes, a translation to pure sound on the way to no-sound-at-all. A medieval score for Vigils, I'm guessing, or a facsimile of one. The initial Hour in the Book of Hours, sung around 3 A.M., Vigils is the first of seven from the Divine Office worked out fully on paper by the thirteenth century. Vigils is not only the first Hour of prayer; it's the oldest, a throwback to the early Church, a precursor to the more commonly sung Matins. Saint Benedict, whose rule the Trappists follow, called it "the night office."

7:30 A.M. in the dining room and it's still December-dark in the huge windows. That rich silence, again. You truly hear it when there are people around who could easily break it to bits. Then, a double-take and the sharp ache of absence in me: the back of a man in a lovingly worn-out Irish fisherman's sweater so like my husband's. Everyone is turned away or to the side, staring off into the void or head down; they read through breakfast, their reflections in those wide, tall windows. Some lift a thin red ribbon, then turn a page. Without the standard talk, talk, talk this public space goes private, ghostly, my compatriots somehow transformed to pure spirit, accommodating no one, their lived lives all to themselves or forgotten this week. *Pax* can get spooky. We're all forgotten here. No obligation to announce ourselves, to give off signals, to establish the usual who-am-I and how and why and what's ahead. A surprise, a relief.

A sign informs me that the bread I eat is made here, by the monks. I accidentally toast it to nearly black. Savor the ashes, I tell myself in a flash of high drama. Metaphor, metaphor. Really? It's all about metaphor, then? Or oxymoron? *Utter silence.* But how can you utter silence?

Back in my room, light floods everything now. Light equals time. Early light means a passing, the invention of verb tense, a widening. The *-ing* form: keep going, friend. Light, the Neolithic reassurance that at some point in the small hours, the world didn't end after all. You think the old *dark as night* but no, it's morning slipping slowly into the world, to make it all visible again. At once, the specifics of what's out there clarify: a path roughly angled uphill between trees to the meadow beyond. No, not all at once: beauty's a crooked, gradual thing from this window. Exactitude and distance, certainty and mystery, close and far. I might as well be talking about poetry.

Then it's more reading, walking, jotting a few notes. Keeping still begins to seem normal, not just a gag order on what I really want to say. I've brought some of Merton's work, though the guesthouse library is filled with it. For someone so keyed to silence, he says a hell of a lot, like, "Nobody started it, nobody is going to stop it. It will talk as long as it wants, this rain." Not yet, not here at the abbey. Too cold for rain. I recheck the schedule. Some of us will be reassembling upstairs in the church for Sext, the fourth office, and the chanting will continue as if never stopped.

Midday rolls around, not lunch but "dinner," that rural tradition my small town grandparents treasured, their "big meal at noon." We line up with our trays for the second time today. Hot soup, that good bread next to a square of butter sized for a giant, left here to share, and the only meal each day that meat is offered. In a while, it's upstairs to the church again, psalms at the Hour of None in a slow ringing out.

Sitting in the back of the church in folding chairs, we're cut off from the monks, who file in singly or in small groups and take their assigned places in pews set perpendicular to us, in two sets that face each other. We watch them in profile, maybe thirty brothers. The ancient call and response starts up again. It must get annoying, even maddening, these rhythmic interruptions in one's working and the day's endless detail, this gathering so often for prayer. Then: no, these monks signed up both to do and to be; this is wholly my quarrel and my complaint. I have their metric perfectly ass-backwards. It's the daily labor that interferes, not the prayer. Point of view is everything. It's *pray always* for these contemplative orders, or so we were told in

Catholic school. Auto-breath, I think. Flesh and blood. Input and output. The tide, shadow of clouds, light on water, then shadow again.

After: the afternoon. More reading, writing, wandering about outside until *locked out*—the key I stupidly left in the room! Then the longer Vespers. Part of Saint Benedict's rule on the Hours is the requirement to stand, mostly. To keep the monk from falling asleep, says a book from the library, a history of the Trappists. Clearly, prayer wears you out, or the workaday stuff *before* prayer does. Eventually, supper. Walking around in my coat, I am saved by a master key lent to me in the kitchen by a woman who lives in town, only turning up to help at meals.

Before we break for the night, a talk from the chaplain, who tells us a painful story of mother and brother to illustrate the difference between a problem to solve and a cross to bear. It comes to me that the thinnest of lines means an ocean to cross. I take that one thought to bed with me.


### Day Three

I decide to walk, to try a *serious* walk with my bum knee, hip, ankle, the latter two still in dire straits even with the help of my trusty hiking poles. Eyeing them as I ask about the trails, a new monk at reception weighs in, worried: Wouldn't it be wise to ask one or two of your fellow residents to go with you?

It's more than hesitation, my thinking *and who in the world might that be?* Surely this guy doesn't imagine we'd break the rule and *talk* to each other? In any case, I'd be intruding on someone else's DIY retreat, his or her dreamwork and inner-space time travel. On such a walk, if only for civility's sake, I'd feel compelled to leave behind this silence that is weirdly rearranging my brain cells—I hope it is, anyway—for the good and for the strange. Is it plain selfishness, my wanting to keep this quietude to myself? I keep rationalizing a kindness in my leaving others to theirs.

I'll be fine by myself, I tell him. I have a cell phone.

They don't work up here, he reminds me.

Right. That *seems* right anyway, in such a place.

All this translates to a shrug, one way to mull over such warnings, though I do take his advice about the hidden door in the distant outer wall to leave the immediate monastery grounds, to cross the road into woods. Twenty-six hundred acres is what they have, an expanse like solace or a very large and radiant secret. It's like my waking to snow earlier, everything covered in its brightness.

That is, until I reach the statues, the destination of this hike. In the woods' dark and deep, I find two larger-than-life bronze sculptures: the first a shrouded woman in great mourning; the second—three figures collapsed against one another, exhausted by grief. We are all left behind eventually.

It's so cold; no place to sit. Occasionally, a bird thinks to sing, then, midway, thinks again. The statues turn everything inward, a new kind of silence. Merton wrote how crucial it was "to be conscious of both extremes of my solitary life, consolation and desolation; understanding, obscurity; obedience and protest; freedom and imprisonment." A longing, a warning. How did he get to that notion? One thing welcomes the next. A flycatcher flicks off a fencepost in "momentary flight." Merton called the bird "an indecipherable ideogram against a void of mist." Or maybe it was the lizard that inspired him; two lizards earlier in that passage holding their ground, staring him down as he entered the hermitage lent to him on the grounds the last eight years of his life.

It's those leaps he makes. Metaphor as a sprung trap working in reverse to release a human thought.

Because it's winter, almost 5 P.M., the day is nearing dark when I return to the monastery. The monk stationed in the reception area where conversation is allowed is speaking to another guest roughly my age, also here for the week; he refers to her as "sister." I wonder which order. As a kid, I had Franciscans, the BVMs (the Sisters of the Blessed Virgin Mary), and the Mercy nuns, three different schools following three different family moves, kindergarten through twelfth grade.

You know who this is? the monk asks me. She wrote *Dead Man Walking.*

Later, after supper, it's Compline, the last set of prayers and the longest, which ends the day and draws night closer. Many of us attend. The chanting finished, we're signaled through the gate to follow the monks down the main aisle to be blessed by the Abbot, who holds his aspergillum high, a silver rattle of sorts, winging it over us in a one-by-one rhythm of *you, whoever you are,* and *now you,* and *now you*. The holy water of my childhood flicks out, the cool and strange startle of it.

And so we enter what the Trappists call "the great silence"—sleep, its night, its depth, its angels and demons, all the way to morning. Or not exactly morning as we know it because—

### Day Four

Two strangers and me. Only three of us make it to the 3:15 A.M. Vigils, those first prayers of the day, and like Compline they take nearly an hour. A thick, near total darkness in the church then *click*, abrupt lights reveal the monks filing in. These morning psalms, not unlike the other Hours, are mostly grim—ungodly Godly threats, promises of bloody resolve to defend the Chosen, the Old Testament at its fiercest. I wonder if this is it, those huge pages that transfixed me in the library, pulled from someone's head centuries ago, a page of this score sung now by a only a few monks, then a response to that call from the rest of the brothers, including our motley crew seated downwind, sleepy behind the separating gate. Outside in the weather, it's the ancient death wish straight, at least a moonless warm-up for the end, a pantomime in December's cold. Inside, beyond this lit high-ceiling room, still the living, breathing death that sleep is for most of us.

Then I'm back there, too, in bed until breakfast, skipping Lauds at 5:45 A.M.

Later, at the guesthouse library, I read again about the history of this most revered of contemplative orders, a breakaway group of the Cistercians established at La Trappe, France, in 1664. The Trappists embraced greater austerity and commitment, something closer to the bone of a first faith, a strict observance of the radical ideas of Saint Benedict. An added vow: beyond the classic chastity, poverty, and obedience is *stability*, meaning the abbey one enters, one leaves by dying. The chants at the Hours are tuneless, merely a powerful shift of key that keeps rising and falling on a seemingly endless repeat. Which is to say: Stay put, share this common life.

I keep coming back to Thomas Merton, his meditations on the natural world, edited as a daybook of sorts. I take it with me to meals and lay it open, next to my plate, morphing into one of those earnest sorts in the dining room who read while they eat. Among so much that stops me, this, not about birds or clouds or stars, and certainly not the common life at all. More and more, over time, his sense of the "common life" began to go beyond the monastery and into the world stricken by war, poverty, injustice. And given the growing scrutiny of his Trappist superiors, he became more and more careful about how he spoke and wrote about such things. Protest could be a meditation, cultural analysis certainly a part of that, prayer even. But in public? Anywhere on the planet, by whatever means, the responsibility deepens and "the poet finds himself where I am," he wrote. That would be "alone, silent . . . careful not to say what he does not mean" or to put out there "what another wants him to say."

In other words, Merton was open to an open mind. *Poet*, Merton wrote. Poetry: what silence makes to aid and abet whatever ends up on the page. Poetry: this very particular *not* saying but fully attentive to the detail and finally the larger picture those details reveal.

Such willful busy quiet is gradual and puzzling, probably never complete, even here, in the monastery. There's a Trappist sign language I've been reading about, and isn't reading itself a form of human speech? Some smile at me as they pass in the dining room, in the hallways, or outside on the trails. And I nod back. Silence has a way of parsing all this.

Today the monk taking a turn at reception, where conversation is allowed, is the one who welcomed me that first night. I ask him about the Order's tradition of sign language. Is it only the basic stuff? Merely functional, as the books claim? Like, *Hand me that hammer, would you?* Or, *Any water to spare?*

Well, mainly yes, it does work the bare minimum, he says, but sometimes . . .

He pauses—should he reveal this to the likes of me? And with his left hand hits the knuckle of his right index finger, then taps the side of his head.

Know what that means?

Nope.

*Knucklehead!* We have other gestures for that, too.

Sort of like the Inuit's many words for snow?

His face lights up. I've found a fellow wise guy! Brother Gerlac is bent, clearly a bad back (no doubt the source of honest agony) but he's wryly, happily on the mark. He entered the Trappists in 1958 as a young man. I ask him about the violence of the sung Psalms in so many of the Hours. It's just that the psalms I recall from my years of belief decades ago were pretty upbeat, full of praise and glory, even delight. I could be misremembering. The question floats there between us: Why the really gruesome ones?

We don't always sing every word, he says pointedly.

I take another big hike today, this time to the Stone House, a hermitage in disrepair, about a mile in and a mile back, quite a trek for me these days. I know my leg and ankle will pay for this. Sometimes pain is worth the pain, I lecture myself. And the place is, in fact, beautiful and moving in the way partial ruins often are, all past and to come hopelessly and darkly intermixed, the door of this cottage held shut with a large branch propped up against the broken latch. An old spiral notebook, a ballpoint pen ready on a table in its one room so hikers can leave thoughts. For years I've been—and still am—as comfortably lapsed as any cradle Catholic might become, but in those pages of pious realizations from other pilgrims, I leave my favorite passage from the poet George Oppen. It may as well be prayer.

*Love of the world, it's not a sunny day in the country. It is the love of fate.*

### Day Five

I'm meant to check out by 8 A.M. on Friday. After breakfast, as outlaws in this silent dining room, Helen Prejean and I finally exchange a few more words. She's written a wildly important book, and we haven't spoken since the reception-area monk introduced us. I repeat the Oppen line that keeps at me, the one I left at the Stone House; it could be she'll find something in it. She volunteers her email address. I'll send her other fragments I cherish from Oppen's daybook. But I don't say so, just promise myself soon, when I get home—

By 8 A.M., I am packed and ready to launch. Do I have nothing to show for my days and nights here? This place, where silence is a timelessness, an always-was, a waiting, a richness, a quiet, a blank. And if I never fill it? No rise and fall to this story.

The long trip back, stepping into my car—that peculiar American solitude—strikes me suddenly as odd.

*Cold. Car. Take it out of park and into drive.*

It isn't that simple, is it? This minute and the next and the next . . .

A stillness moving through space is all.

# THE BURNING

⌣

COVID. The sorrow doesn't stop.

The best escapes from lockdown meant walks in the woods. I can praise our favorite trails or new lush spots that friends in our small pod have shown us. Spring! Into summer! Time passes. Those silent birds with nothing to say in March now sing out of lust for off-spring or territory, first wildflowers like bloodroot, jack-in-the-pulpit, trillium come and gone, sunlight in the leafed-out trees a dappled flourish. I've learned new things from field guides long ignored, such as the diameter of the maple tree out back makes it one hundred and fifty years old. One foot equals a half century. (Happy birthday!) For a while, I told everyone: Guess the natural world didn't get the COVID memo. A lovely spring, I said ad nauseam, in glad disbelief. *A little coolish*, my mother would've put it, if she still could.

Of course we've paid some attention—in poetry and beyond—to the natural world, since Pliny the Elder at least, his death 70 C.E., thereabouts. Here's the end of his bio: after writing the thirty-seven books of his *Naturalis Historia*, the most exhaustive study we have from the Ancients, no bestiary stranger or more surreal, Pliny died near Pompeii of fumes from the fiery rain of Vesuvius. That famously food-loving genius insomniac heroically crossed the Bay of Naples in a small boat to rescue a friend in the direct line of a volcanic eruption that would bury two cities. As for his *Natural History*, I suspect the curious Pliny would have given a lot to add Australia to his every-where hoard of everything. Such astonishing wildlife there, science still perplexed at how such oddities got to that remarkable continent. (Ask the Indigenous elders, I want to say.)

I mention Australia because I spent five months there on a Fulbright in 2019, observing kangaroos, wallabies, emus, and koalas and preparing to write my own bestiary. That quirky and capable, however ancient, Pliny, first *looker* (and imaginer), somehow ended up in those poems as fuse and startle, a now and then forget-me-not though I didn't fully invite him. It's how poems work, laying claim and then losing track of stumbled but well-meaning starts, intention itself not worth much.

My begging bowl from Australia overfloweth with mythic strangeness. After we left, the real heartbreak began, great fires ravishing thousands of hectares, over three billion beloved animals burned alive or starved to rag and bone, their habitats in ruin. A grief, a hall of mirrors of grief, a whole outback of grief, multiple reefs of grief, one smoky borderless cloud of grief. Terrible footage on American television and news websites; terrible emails from friends in Australia. Days ashy as night, people going to bed in gas masks, knitting mittens for burnt koalas. At Tidbinbilla, the nature reserve near Canberra, the wonders my husband and I as volunteers saw—platypus, black swans, those koalas, a wily one-winged pelican—packed up and moved out of the line of, literally, fire. Some of them. Some.

Even a quick scan of the world's recent natural history is alarming but given climate's disastrous changes, our moment continues to feel so end-of-it, like COVID itself. And the red-hot burn-alert during that period from Australia fast became world prophecy. Well into February of that subsequent year, 2020, even at a distance and an ocean between, the horrific light of those flames darkened each poem coming out of me that became a collection, *Bestiary Dark*. Correction: those poems came *through* me, my attempt to put words on a page a *means*, not a *source*. All poets, I think, understand that drill.

I hesitate to say *all poets*. All *anything*, for that matter. Uncertainty and mystery make background music for poetry's radar held out to collect what images of the world fall our way. But tragic times take such a bowl back to the potter's wheel, hands full of mud and water, time given to shaping something that will harden to the *made* thing in the searing kiln. A specific how-to: you lean *in* is what I remember as the soggy mess threatens every second to spin off the wheel and all over me. After each day at the wheel years ago, I biked home soaked in clay, in *earth*, most profound stuff of the planet, my jeans and shirt drying thick with it. An elemental self-realization of sorts. *Dust to dust. Through a glass darkly.* Okay.

It's analogy then, to say our pandemic carried, and still carries, a similar inflation and reduction within its narrative, this COVID-19 and its offspring with infectious microscopic agents of fear and possible death by way of what comes out of human lungs when anyone says hello. On go the masks for any planned or chance encounter. You can't wait to get back to the car after a grocery run—to remove it. *Couldn't* wait, and probably will go through it again. A deep breath is loving air unhindered.

Writing that bestiary did the crucial proverbial *thing* for me, the strange turning familiar, the familiar strange, until it scared me—beauty intensified by the threatened state of so much: the brush-tailed rock wallaby, only eighty or so left in the world, or the ancient rivers and streams dried to dusty ribbons in a seemingly perpetual drought, brittle eucalyptus and scrub poised to fuel the fires to come, the gorgeous endless desolation of the outback we circled in a rented yellow car our final thirty days in Australia. As we began that drive in late June 2019 toward the storied, dreaded Nullarbor Plain and parts west then north, then straight down through the middle of a continent, a friend—exasperated and worried—kept warning us: *nothing to see!*

No, not nothing. Look into a favorite poem for practice. It's vast in there too. Or consider the death counts from COVID-19 on the evening news, lives lived behind numbers.

We can bad-dream backwards. Pliny began the first book of his *Natural History* with a question carried out from the ancient world that burns in my bestiary's prologue because—full disclosure—I did invite him in after all, and struck his five words like a match, trying to light my book: *The world, is it finite?* A question anyone facing a pandemic, or the die-off of so many species, must feel. And don't all questions burn?

Poetry goes sideways to suggest, to layer up, to connect. We digress to think clearly by imagining *like, as, is*, the great equations, a redefinition. The leap is metaphoric, what makes a poet *a poet*, said Aristotle, of whom Pliny was wildly jealous, the standard admiring (and witty, and disdainful) Roman take on the Greek intelligentsia, the ones who got there first and so gracefully.

We can read earlier eras like a mirror or crystal ball, and other poems shadowed by *grim*, if only for company during our pandemic, bodies burning up with fever and secreted from families, the contagion and lists of those who haven't survived announced daily. I continually think of Ellen Bryant Voigt's *Kyrie*, published 1995 in the wake of AIDS though brilliantly focused on the 1918 influenza pandemic that wiped out millions worldwide.

> You wiped a fever-brow, you.
> You scrubbed a sickroom floor, you burned the mop.
> What wouldn't burn you boiled like applesauce
> out beside the shed in the copper pot.

There's burning, a burning *past*, into a future. Our own temperatures could shoot up for days on end in the months ahead.

A finite thing or not, the writing we do—

# BOREDOM

⌒

I like when boredom is forgiving, passing out of itself for a moment. A rather bland afternoon mid-June, for instance. Which could be yesterday, when the Future Farmers of America kids came flooding the campus where I teach, emptied now because classes are out. Suddenly, hundreds of dark blue jackets everywhere, gold FFA letters on them, and later, three high school girls on a break from whatever the Future Farmers have gathered here to do, wildly giggling between bursts of not-quite-words. I saw them walking near the university through the so-called village with its trinket shops, its fast food and beer joints, past Von's, best independent bookstore in the Midwest. Maybe the girls should have been back at one of the Student Union's conference rooms, taking notes, alert to a new pesticide's murderous wonders. Sure, they were playing hooky, their jackets at an angle almost jaunty. One can hope.

Not much could be more out of sync in the current culture of hip-hearted teens than Future Farmers of America, even in rural midwestern America where I live. And bully for them! I love their oddity, the dull stamped-in serious sameness of the jacket, its ungendered attempt at an outcome, a place. Those girls, nevertheless, seemed specifically themselves, whoever that is or may be, come such a future. At that moment, they were loudly amused, each at a different key and duration, having loosened their ties, and their collars open and their first shirt button unbuttoned. They kept walking, and laughing.

How this connects to poetry, I don't know yet. But let's be clear: boredom opens things up. There's solace in that openness, thick as syrup. It knows the end before whatever happens gets underway, so cool about nearly all, but not everything. There's a leftover spill, and that spill is poetry. Those girls were free in flight for the moment, because of their boredom. They'd gone AWOL.

---

I'm an expert on boredom, though perhaps not the kind so sure of itself. Evidence: I survived grade school. Most of us do. Think of the near-decade passed in those places. So little remembered, although there's clear proof something happened: one writes a sentence, after all; one can read what others write. Both are triumphs, mysterious and not exactly small.

In my case, a horde of baby boomers at St. Eugene's School, some fifty of us filled each class, a single officious nun to wrangle us in. Weeks and years in those rooms, like weather—a vast cloud that darkens yard to street to playground, a few steps, a door, boredom washing over as others stood and recited or went to the blackboard to diagram subject past verb to object and beware the dangling modifier. So many of us. One could hide there.

For those who came after: the time-out chair. Minutes into more minutes and maybe a lifetime-so-far sends you to sit and stare. *I want you to think about what you've done.* So goes a voice several feet higher as you look straight ahead, right into the poem. It's never what you've done. And guilt? Boredom erases as secretly as the poem erases, you name it—intention, the self, what one should be doing. A relief and a leveling to be in that corner where the world pretty much forgets you.

The radiator droned on. We were orderly in our classroom, needle-quiet. Nothing for it but to go solitary and inward—where else?—and thus, the imaginative life begins.

Praise boredom, crucial backdrop and trigger.

---

It must be said that boredom is a luxury. Who could be bored in a village—your village—shelled by insurgents or government troops? Is that flippant to say? Boredom says it.

Other things unspeakable: a tsunami, a fire, a flood, a tornado. Their aftermath's lower grade of panic, the making-do, the endless hard stretch suddenly ahead, platitudes repeated ad nauseum until your eyes roll back: boredom winnows through.

You're a sieve for it, then a vessel. You rest briefly in its rootless half-sleep. Put *poetry* in that place with *vessel, briefly, endless, sieve.*

———

Most mornings in the coming-out-of-dark, before whatever words turn up on the page, I get the kettle going. I lay the tea bags in a small metal pot. There's steaming water to pour, my finger at the rim in such little light, waiting for the heat and the pinch to gauge how close. I almost always think of Marianne Moore, her writing somewhere about the blind woman who did this to figure how much, when to stop. I do stop, and flip shut the hinged lid. Day after day, this touch and this thought. Boredom isn't monotony, isn't depression, is a sweet and stinging strangeness in between.

———

If a poet—say it's Auden—stares at a painting until there is nothing for him in the world but that painting, is it boredom or is it love? I could stand still as Lady Justice, eyes bandaged up for the job, arm raised with the balance: Breugel's *Landscape with the Fall of Icarus* in the left silver scale, Auden's *Musée des Beaux Arts* in the right. Which one would—what? Win? Be sentenced to hard labor? And is the winner the lighter or the heavier, fuller of wonder or more grief-struck?

Because the ploughman in poem or painting, the shepherd at the edge of the water both look away too and do what they do in silence. Boredom is that removed, its arrogant and fragile boy aloft.

———

Are the dead bored beyond astonishment? Have they passed to indifference? If they are and have, who writes the poems to be written, who stains the place left blank as a box minus its pins?

My grandfather, decades gone. One night, after surgery, on narcotics for pain, I dream his room back. Some work's been done since his death; past the towering desk, the ticking clock, a new hallway put in. I walk, then turn and there he is, in the same straight-backed chair.

*Beebop! Have you been here all this time?*

It's my voice in the dream, caught in our old endearment for him, crying out to his half smile, his bare nod, vacant years of nothing but *wait* all over him. Finally, no finally. It's like he—the both of us— never left 1965 though I am *now*, I am older. Big deal. So what, says his patient boredom, a higher form of it of it than mine.

There are moments boredom unknowns all: I could, but I won't. Not *unable*. Not *forever thus*. Just stop me before I *narrative* again, before I make shape over time to end lyric time. An emphatic *will not* a defense, its *do not* already at a distance.

*I do not go from home*, Emily Dickinson said, where boredom reigned—her house a gated community, her open window from which she lobbed poem and poem and poem.

It's tradition, a kind of daydream drill: a long solo stretch on an island eventually occurs to us. Merely the thought of it—"my happy place," says a friend hemmed in on all sides by husband and children. Island and self, serenely deserted. To have time to be bored! Forget questions of food or drink.

Such an exile comes with one rousing, single-minded cliché: what book to bring, what piece of music, as if love is a contest and the prize is you stranded with the last and best of the planet. I rarely believe those who say Proust, *I'd bring Proust!* But how Whitman's beard would keep growing there, a real measure of time passing.

About his island, Elizabeth Bishop's Crusoe remembers the smallest things lit, a knife, for instance, and "how many years did I / beg, implore it, not to break?"—as boredom rose and fell, in and out of dreams of "other islands / . . . infinities / of islands, islands spanning islands." Endurance, then melancholy, is a drug. It's after the fact in Bishop's poem, a giving up that gives way. Crusoe post-rescue, back in England, where he recedes to quite another lift and dark, "drinking my real tea."

Boredom as sea-wash. It expands, it contracts.

Meanwhile, every meanwhile reveres the longing involved. But longing forgets, boredom its own bound copy of single-celled words until even they withdraw. To where? The sun is terrible in poems. All you think of is shade on such islands, whatever final book you bring. Boredom: the sequel, the sequel, the sequel.

---

Those silly-earnest old films, black-and-white, where most everyone smokes cigarettes and drinks martinis and stays inside. The room is comfortable, a fire lit and crackling.

Darling, she says, I've gone mad with boredom.

Sound *tells*. It's a line of living heartbeat on a screen, a *Reader's Digest* condensed book. Her come-hither trochee—*Dár-ling*—morphs to *I've gone mad*, three stalled stresses miming loss before her trochaic return to finish, to keep going some of that. *Bóre-dom*: you step down hard, first syllable, before it floats up.

Melodrama aside, it's my brother circa 1962, coming into the house partway through the movie, already bored unto smart-ass after watching two minutes. Who's right? he says.

*I am.* That was our mother, her sane and comic two-beat mode.

---

Russell Edson, so succinct on matters of hover and dream off. I paraphrase, sort of: A man builds a house. He's so eager! It's a complete mess right now of blueprint, struts and nails, brick and more brick. *But between the plan and the finished house, there is a terrible span of boredom.* A deep breath in that, and from that. *Perhaps his unfinished house is a language . . .*

---

Here's the honest-to-god entry I found in my Webster's, a book that's falling apart. For "–dom," a suffix: "ME, fr. OE -*dōm*: akin to OHG -*tuom -dom*, OE *dōm*, judgment," in stately brackets. You go back the way poetry goes back to figure out what it means, things beneath, in spite of. So many *doms* making for bigger-than-big, for mock-heroic: Anglo-Saxon*dom*, duke*dom*, official*dom*. But *freedom*, too, says the dictionary, and *kingdom* among those states of realm, of office, of being. *Boredom* listed there—no, not its patient, low-pressure reach.

To repeat: Middle English, check. And certainly Old High German, Old English where "dom" equals *judgment*. From such a height, boredom looks down, into a future.

———

The late 1970s, early '80s, and still. And still! Skinny female models in slick magazines turned fierce, scary even. Like blood, the first time you smell iron in it. They stand aloof, bored to smithereens at the edge of a damaged world, marooned in new clothes. A kind of faux-boredom, though not entirely, not the *seeming* that once triggered our old neighbor's lively scorn for men who undid their top two buttons, so pointedly rakish, so look-at-me. "Affecting an open shirt" our old neighbor Allison Cook liked to tell us.

But the young models in the ads, their *couldn't care less*, leaned toward and away. Sorrow so detached from its source becomes abandon and ice and curiously free. The shock of Louise Glück writing those early poems where Gretel says to Hansel, *I killed for you*, or a voice out of the ether takes flowers long past their pretty givens—*I hate them. / I hate them as I hate sex. . . .* A blunt and abruptly released austerity in such phrases, too assured, too beautiful. The look in those models' eyes: *I dare you.*

It isn't hate, too much flat-lining in it, too much long view.

———

Boredom. Post-boredom. It still amounts to staging. No, the poem need not moral-tale us or make us love the poet. Poem ≠ anything in particular. A good doggy in each one, not required. There's room.

We all live a life. It never comes to a point. Ask Philip Larkin, snarky and exhausted, brilliantly miserable. Get him up on the Ouija board.

Somewhere, Yeats advises following a tense line with a numb line. *Numb* might be a word for boredom that ends badly. For *numb* then *tense*, two words: *Sylvia Plath*.

# THE OTHER WORDSWORTH

In 2012, in Scotland because I was a Fulbright Professor at the University of Edinburgh and also a Fellow at their Institute for Applied Study in the Humanities—wild dumb luck on both counts—I took the train down to Grasmere for the Wordsworth Trust's Festival of Women's Poetry at Dove Cottage, at first simply grateful for more rare luck: the chance to see the UK's three Laureates at the time—Carol Ann Duffy, Liz Lochhead, and Gillian Clarke. That turned out to be rewarding enough. What I didn't expect was that at one point I'd sit in a room full of poets and hear of the hidden heroics of Dorothy Wordsworth.

A small, brooch-at-the-collar older woman stood at the lectern and we all leaned forward like young birds waiting to be fed. I'm not young so forgive that analogy, but there was something so immediately engaging about Pamela Woof—her warmth, her meticulous good sense, her no-nonsense passion for the letters and journals she had edited—that won us over from the start: *Will you adopt me? Right now? On the spot?* Or so I imagined. But surely, she has her own daughters, I thought then, coming back to earth, back to reason. Still, that old expression—*we hung on every word*—is sometimes true.

What little I already knew about Dorothy Wordsworth is the backbone of this: She'd lost her teeth fairly early and so dodged any likeness to be made of her after that. She walked long miles in the Grasmere hills, exactly as her famous brother did and against the knee-jerk disapproval of the day, women being the fragile creatures they were and, probably in many minds, still are. Dorothy kept a garden of both domestic and wild flowers. And, of course, the fact is there *were* her journals, which no doubt William read. How many of his sister's fine observations on the page or in the air as they talked did he lift whole cloth?

Those journals! Which were what our brilliant speaker, Pamela Woof, talked of and into that hour at the festival. Thus, our lean forward, an instant engagement with this village explainer of many remarkables concerning the life and work of this *other* Wordsworth. My memory fogs up but I do recall the thrill that ran through that audience as Woof explored the power of *image* for this writer, her ahead-of-her-time habit of looking and then recording so clearly the daily concrete particulars of her world.

I see this as a kind of impatience with the philosophical overlay of the Romantics, the thousand-pound weight of abstraction expected of "serious" writers to move quickly past the *thing* into what it means spelled out, not allowed to suggest, to come gradually into a more layered resonance. In May 1800, for instance, she wrote, "As I was going out in the morning I met a half crazy old man. He shewed me a pincushion, & begged a pin." *In the moment* is what we might call it now, and how that defines Dorothy Wordsworth's painterly way with image in the journals, an approach that wouldn't come into poetry in earnest, with such willfulness, until a young Ezra Pound began his ranting and cruise-directing nearly a century later. The only poet never to belittle William Blake in those years of the Romantics, even seeking him out once for a long walk, it was Coleridge who knew what Dorothy Wordsworth was up to at Dove Cottage (or so I've read). And of her own sorrow: "Grasmere was very solemn in the last glimpse of twilight it calls the home to quietness . . . I could not keep the tears within me."

I took many notes during that talk—the way image works; how it haunts and continues; how it is often unconscious, but comes from a lived life and, mainly, privations in childhood; the notion of fire, for instance, its fevered, wished-for solace recurring in those journals. How memorable image emerges from danger, threats to the self, the way prey senses the predator and acts accordingly. Pamela Woof linked this unsung Wordsworth and her alert eye for image with the early loss of the family's mother, and as the only daughter, how she was sent away to live with others and never a hearth in her room. So many references in those journals to a chill that pierces and numbs. Does such cold ever leave us? Listening so keenly to this scholar and critic, we were poets suddenly moved, then wondering or worried, tracing back those images which keep coming up from the dark of our own work to haunt, pin down, scare us.

Danger or *in* danger. So many dangers to live through, speak to, suppress, only to have them return over and over as images in one's dreams or one's poems or one's journals. Out there, in here, staying put, going forward, being the many or the one frozen before the wonders or many griefs of the world. And to *be* dangerous? You *say* such things, or *write* them. But first—

Shrug, says Dorothy Wordsworth. I keep hearing her: *walk around.*

# SECRET LIFE

⌐

Line. Of course—the major element in the great divide between poetry and prose, one of those first-glance definitions: a set of lines might well *equal* poem, no matter what those lines contain. But this notion misleads. After all, it has been said endlessly that prose "chopped up into lines" isn't necessarily a poem. And poems do occur without lines, sometimes even outside of poetry itself, if we are to believe Wallace Stevens on the subject.

Still. Still, the presence of line is a key reason poems *mime*, on the page, what's true, meaning what complicates, and therefore what resembles things as they really are. For starters, line is an architectural device that suggests what is profoundly interior, bringing up pause, hesitation, the heard and visual sense—*oh, I get it*—of something coming into being, right now. That interiority works directly against the bright-light, rational feel of the sentence—the very *public* sentence threaded down the page to make those lines.

It's ironic. The famously secret life of the poem is both revealed and protected by that good-doggy social contract of the complete sentence (oh, hard-working subject, verb, object!), even the ghost of one, via the fragment. The line, against the larger wealth of the sentence, is a rebel thing which undercuts order. With it comes all that can't be fully controlled: the irrational, the near-deranged, the deeply personal and individual utterance. Thus, poetry. And the line—kept *almost* in line by the commonplace raised-right sentence—enacts its own drama, in direct cahoots with the strange, the unending.

# AUDIO

⌒

A scraping outside, preparations for painting the house, or obsessive whatever sparrow / cardinal / wren (*here: drink this, drink this, drink this*), the sound of making and remaking.

Tiny happenstance creature in the wall—hear that? Then, reverse to a given, a routine: so many pencils on the move in life drawing class, urgent whish and waft, the sound of total attention. Tree branches in wind, Earth spinning, rivers rivering, a key in a lock, syncopation of thunder and lightning, backfiring trucks. The holy rumble of contemplatives for life, the 3 A.M. chill, the dark prayerful *repeatable* of those women convincing themselves, convincing themselves, growing old.

Chant, white noise to fake an ocean. We winnow grief and relief into wiry couplets, lush stanzas, stories that fit the mind then vanish into supper, night, the next day, a just-in-time siren, the ambulance, each groan and whimper locked in steel and the jostle, twenty blocks to go. Refrigerator hum, the *icebox* she still called it midcentury, low ringing in the ear, Keats walking through the early morning streets reading his "Ode to a Nightingale" aloud, then Whitman, hospital volunteer, 1864, listening to time itself while the wounded soldiers slept.

Say the poetry in everything is simple: a *descending*. You can hear it. Babies in tears, kids whining at the checkout for a sweet taste, a boy stroking a cat, the cat's purr of pleasure (*be gentle, be gentle*), adolescents in love with exquisite disdain, an unrehearsed flood of

words then the cutting pause and pause to *Jesus, do you believe that?*
Thrilling—

———

Thus, overture, where even silence is sound. The long day settles,
wears out. *A musical idea* equals "to repeat is to make memorable," a
composer told me, a eureka moment I keep quoting. And tell, retell
my treasured blip of story, someone else writing a—*quartet?*

I breathed. *Wow, what's that like?*

*It's solving one little problem after another.* A shrug the composer
released out loud.

"Thought tends to collect in pools," says Wallace Stevens, my
favorite claim of his to repeat. Because pools of thought can clear
and cloud, regrettable, unstoppable; they have a soundtrack. A voice
under and over racing ahead, held back for the next chance to speak.
You can't hear everything at once. Conversation is—what?—20 or
30 percent not-quite-listening? You drift inward and out for context
personal and distant, a perspective.

Think that word *ambulance* full of oxygen's hiss, frantic *yeah, here,
god no, look at me, we're fine, we're fine,* the speeding cramped quarters, time in the freeze mode. I repeat: to repeat is to make memorable.
Poetry's grief and relief might talk to each other early morning, or at
night, for weeks or years. To recall is to blur into sepia the *was* and
*right now* and *what's to come.*

———

An old friend, Marea Gordett, once insisted that Emily Dickinson
"rhymed" when she did not, at least not in any usual way. In Amherst,
a century and a half ago, Marea said, the poet turned rhyme sideways, upside down, for whatever sort of *joining*. I'll never be fully sold
on the notion though such eccentricity is irresistible. You blink, and
blink again. How much doubles, layers up, compounds. Because time
moves forward and in reverse, I like to back into a ten-year-old me,
watching my mother not yet my age in a photograph holding a bat,
ready to swing. That moment I've ached to enter, walking right into
the frame to rhyme my life with hers in some pre-birth netherworld.

It's not that I like baseball, I'd tell her; my job is to wait two decades right here. The look she'd give me: that silence is huge. Mid-morning, 1930. Birdsong close, an owl confused by daylight or a thrush too early, its late afternoon song anyway, kids shouting in the middle distance.

Even now I hear such things though my family's eventual habit is *go deaf,* half the time *excuse me, what?* for years. . . . Which is the history of refrain, isn't it? And persistence. And longing. *To rhyme my life with hers.* Is it simply a matter of metaphor? Am I really *like* her? No, but it's my mother again, quieted for the pitch. My walking repeatedly into that photo. A visitation, a cherished coming and going.

My brother calculates with fancy equipment the loss for twenty-year-olds versus forty-year-olds versus those far longer-in-the-tooth, what we hear or not, any of us still underfoot at the party. I lose the ends of words and phrases now, whole syllables drop out mid-talk-talk-talk. Those empty whiplashed patches mean indifference and release (I give up, drift off) or shame. Or, they mute a brain into despair. Was that the draw for Dickinson, so smitten with agony and what is lost? To hold on to lament, death her "flood subject," to salvage or solace by repeating something, a keening by way of the weirdest rhymes she couldn't help herself from making—sounds close enough to catch, to flame up. You turn your head, strain into hope and even joy, because the world does connect and turn familiar, doesn't it? Oh, the nice dinner party of that!

Unless it gets too familiar, as in her dogged *stay put / same exact word* thing—even in this later stanza from her #712, worn smooth by countless readers:

> We paused before a House that seemed
> A Swelling of the Ground—
> The Roof was scarcely visible—
> The Cornice—in the Ground—

So odd. Not so much her end-stopping at "Ground." But skip a line and it's "ground" as end-stop again! That's *rhyme?* What? To recycle both word and placement of word? Pretty dodgy. . . . But that's a sort of metrical fiddling my friend Marea saw in Dickinson. I suppose legit, if only in name, officially "identical rhyme" on the books. (What books? Who makes these rules and names these names?) Well, okay. The dead-ringer bits underscore and insist like some crazy *figure-it-out* impulse in us, buzzing over and over even in sleep to make it crucial. That's how we talk to ourselves and to each other to keep upright, isn't it? (Buck up! Cajole! Forgive!) *To repeat is to make memorable*—and make sense, if luck holds—to aim at that "one little problem after another."

Or, it's truly bleak. The powerful end position in a line whacked once by Dickinson in this piece, twice with a hammer, two stabs, two single-stressed claims. *Ground.* Take that. Then a second blow. And since the ear does crave difference, this poet's cranky repeat puts the onus on the only thing in the phrase that does change. The ear goes right for that: her "of" in a half-second swap for that dark and final "in"—"*in* the ground"—which now leaps out to reveal the real grave she's describing, singular and chilling, qualities there from the start in a poem that famously begins "Because I could not stop for Death / He kindly stopped for me."

Maybe my friend was most taken by another echo, Dickinson's so-called eye rhyme, a twinning only evident on the page itself. The yoking of "one" and "stone" in #303 is an example, or "prove" and "love" in #580. No ear worth its salt or secrets would buy either as an instance of rhyme. It may look the part but—poseurs!—doesn't sound it, though perhaps to believe *is* to see. As with hearing, with sight, too: we can't grasp everything at once. I clearly recall Russell Edson telling me, "I don't think poetry's a literary art at all, do you? It's a visual art." He was at my university for a reading, walking toward the sun. He had just pointed back to his shadow: "Why is that thing following me?"

———

To rhyme one life with another. The noisy stillness in a speeding ambulance. *Relief* and *grief* cross-hatched, the beginning of poetry. Best if it sneaks up—surprise!—just when you didn't expect intimacy, this double-take and times-two. Best as trace, "internal rhyme" slipping into a kind of half-rhyme daydream. I call it *spot rhyme*, a near-disconnect which drifts in seemingly at random to sweeten or nail down and scare a second thought, my favorite audio grace.

It took me years to *hear* these lines I should have loved since I first loved poems, from Dickinson's spooky #812, haunted strange accident, a doorway into—*What is it?* this thing that

> . . . waits upon the Lawn,
> It shows the furthest Tree
> Upon the furthest Slope you know
> It almost speaks to you.

# ADVERBS OR NOT

Since lockdown, and now with its loosening and the governors declaring, for good or ill, their *phases* for reopening stores and restaurants—a sliver, then halfsies, then full-faced as the moon—I've been dreaming madly. Not just that, but the dreams come strangely, rarely sweetly, mostly horribly. Deeply, deeply, deeply is how I sleep these nights. Note the big *ly* trailing behind so many words in these last two sentences, doing its job to connote and drum up meaning via a sideways glance.

To calm myself, I've looked into the adverb as institution, not mere linguistic flourish. This curious part of speech is defined in my grade school's *Voyages in English* as if we were on murky waters, staring up at dim stars while any adverb worth its verb drives our boat of dreams and fine-tunes. Whoever the author-guardians explaining away those voyages were, they got emphatic about one thing: adverbs answer questions. Of time—"when, how often?" (Answer: *again, before, earlier, soon, now*). Or, of place (how about *above, away, below, down, overhead*). Then, "degree" comes into it, "how much or how little" (as in: *almost, quite, rather, very*).

Most dramatically the world is nuanced by that polite but bullying *ly* tacked on as an ending syllable. "Adverbs of manner," my old textbook calls them in its "CLASSIFICATION OF ADVERBS" (for instance: *easily, fervently, quickly, thoroughly*). Mostly glad states of being. But how about *suspiciously, gruesomely, unbelievably, hopelessly, brokenheartedly?* Who knew a book about the wiles and ways of the English language published in 1951, and still hauled out when I hit eighth grade eleven years later, would be rose-coloring fate for its young readers? Maybe that's good to do, upbeat as hope because it *is* hope. As in: the world (keeps) turning—to half-evoke a popular soap opera of that era watched and loved by my stay-at-home mother as she settled in before the TV for her lunch of canned peaches and cottage cheese.

I must be thinking about poetry all the time now, given my mulling over such things through our day after day of rising then falling then rising death counts from COVID, an endless ritual of the unnerved to note those numbers. Meanwhile, I keep giving in to my unconscious each night, all this woven into and playing out in the wee hours to make terrible dreams. A friend, a writer in New York, emails me that she *should* be writing but isn't. Two others admit the same on Zoom. Another writes that he cannot face poetry, his or anyone else's. Take heart, I want to tell them—I don't know—something like: We have the rest of our lives ahead of us, right?

No, not right. And never as easy as cliché would have it, to soothe despair.

Nevertheless, the little workaholic adverb is still at it, framed and semi-fossilized in its full chapter (pages 348–58) in my *Voyages in English*, fifteen well-meaning numbered examples displaying its chops. Our teachers said what mattered was *usage*, habit and its matter-of-fact *how* a crucial part of understanding anything, like a bicycle chain engaged, right foot down, then the left, to make that spare brilliant machine get you someplace. It's as common as sense could be, the adverb's shade and tweaking to charge even the fuzzy past and future into an edged *right now*, thus these examples:

#2. Breathlessly she pushed the curtains aside.

#3. This task will be rather difficult.

I walk into Kroger in a mad-dash hunting and gathering attempt—my turn this week to go out masked, shopping list in hand, uber-organized, no lollygagging, trying to obey the arrows on the floor: which way in which aisle, up past flour and yeast, down crackers and cocoa, shot like a shiny marble in a human-size pinball machine. My grand feat for the day. My *poem* for the day.

Decades ago, in college, I lived in a tiny upstairs room in a ramshackle house I shared with people, a few I still know. My window looked down to the street. Once, I noticed a housemate talking to a friend outside, nothing special until their gestures shifted unaccountably cartoonish, impossible jerking angles of elbow and head and hand notched up past full speed, gone haywire. That was when I realized *in the dream itself* that I was dreaming what I saw in the street, that this was still a nap, that *I was only dreaming I was awake.* Which shocked me.

I tried to come to, for real. And could not. Tried again. Again. And got scared, then terrified: my god, would I never? Never again, this life I sort of loved and sort of didn't? In weird moments, like now, I wonder if any of that was my trapdoor into poetry (just open, and fall through . . .), that dream can be realer than real time, or that mystery itself is both *out there* and *in here.* In any case, I woke relieved I hadn't lost my mind, or at least hadn't checked out for good.

The pandemic threat is so alarmingly *not* visible, passed through air or by touch; it might well be imaginary. Except for heartbreaking details of true stories, the lives lived on PBS's *NewsHour*, faces and stilled gestures of the beloveds lost to the virus each week (holding a child, laughing at a party) which bring home what is central to poetry, the power of *image* to cherish and continue. But why has that old dream of *caught*, never to wake up, come back to me as the virus is having its lethal way with us? Years ago, Robert Bly held forth about our hesitation in the middle of a poem, how to keep going. You ask yourself: *How many worlds can I visit?*

There are many mantras. I've been told they should be meaningless; the point is repetition into a certain mindlessness (read: timelessness) at the center of the world and the self. Back to chapter 6 in *Voyages in English*, where my poor part of speech still spins through its final category: "Adverbs of affirmation and negation tell whether a fact is true or false" like *yes, no, indeed, doubtless, not.*

#10. The bird was not in its cage.

There's also the adverb's home ground again, of manner and time, the last two examples on that startling list:

#14. I shuddered excessively as I passed the haunted house.

#15. The soul will live forever.

# EVERYTHING ALL AT ONCE

⌒

The thing about Wisława Szymborska is this: range and counter-range, her opening and closing virtually in the same synapse-moment. This happens all the time.

"I prefer Dickens to Dostoyevsky." From a later poem, "Possibilities," this line champions Dickens's expanse and joy-dark complication, yet by mere mention, Dostoyevsky's focus, his narrow depth, still hovers in the same flashing instant—this seems a matter of preference, after all, not out-and-out warfare. Such a line, the fourth chiming element in her long mantra of likes in that poem, shrewdly shows what she's considered and perhaps left behind. Almost.

Because one never knows with Szymborska. "I prefer myself liking people / to myself loving mankind." That's another treasure in "Possibilities," where every declaration is singular and plural, this *and* that, somehow radiantly whatever it is. Which is to say: quirky, modest, solid, but oddly partial and thus fully moving:

> I prefer exceptions.
> I prefer to leave early.
> I prefer talking to doctors about something else.

Like Whitman, Szymborska is in love with repetition, the former serious as a heartbeat. The solace of that, its weight-bearing desire to stay put and keep going, keeps the poem going. But the impulse to reverse—she's smitten with, no, addicted to, those turns.

Rule number one: Szymborska refuses to be bored, or to bore us with anything, especially the pious, the expected, the same-old-same-old press to be delivered unto sainthood before our time—surely one of the perennial dangers of poetry.

Thus her wit, her humor, her distance, her warmth. Thus our never knowing exactly how her surefooted declarative starts will fly off their knobs, step out of their ankle braces.

Sometimes it's huge, the whole world involved, its darkest of darks:

> I prefer the earth in civvies.
> I prefer conquered to conquering armies.
> . . . . . . . . . . . . . . . . . . . . . . . .
> I prefer the hell of chaos to the hell of order.

Sometimes, it's curiously close and long behind us, domestic-sweet:

> I prefer desk drawers.
> I prefer the old fine-lined illustrations.

Szymborska seems so sure of herself, coming down with that heavy stick of anaphora, its literary front-loading. But that thud, that initiating repetition, is tricky. Whatever its certainty, it's also: try again, keep figuring it out. "Poets, if they are to be genuine, must . . . keep repeating 'I don't know,'" she has said, standing warily and cheerful enough in Stockholm to accept her Nobel Prize. Her own poems keep starting up again and again—beginning, middle, end—wherever we find ourselves in them. "I prefer to knock on wood" or "I prefer not to ask how much longer and when" or "I prefer keeping a needle and thread on hand, just in case."

And of poetry itself, one of the most beloved subjects in her long, rich lifetime of work, how it, too, opens and closes:

> I prefer the absurdity of writing poems
> to the absurdity of not writing poems.

Again, no great claim. But thankfully—yes—it will do.

# WILD BLUE YONDER

I am a birder, not a bird. Nevertheless I write poems. And it *is* a kind of singing, though every birder knows that it's mainly male birds (save the fair-minded cardinals and grosbeaks) that hold forth, a rule to which literary culture held its human poets for centuries.

There are categories though, regardless of which gender is permitted to sing. Among birds, we have the Duos, those mating for life; the Solitaries, single by choice most of their days, thank you very much; the Flock Birds—swallows, and those heart-stopping elegant cedar waxwings—ho-hum assuming the whole clan will hunt and gather and even nest together, an in-born habit, a kind of cacophonous repetitive chamber music, when they do sing.

This clumping into groups, or not, seems natural for poets too. Robinson Jeffers, Marianne Moore, Brigit Pegeen Kelly, Robert Hayden, Laura Jensen, Philip Larkin, Rosemary Tonks, and of course, Dickinson, all emphatically or quietly one-offs, our Solitary Creepers, those small thrushes that tear your heart out, circling a single tree as solo figures, scrounging under the bark for breakfast. Meanwhile, the Duos for life, the cardinals or eagles: Robert Bly and James Wright, a vivid emphatic twosome-for-the-art, utter disciples for it once up in Minnesota, digging down for the deep image right there under the surface, to reveal a startling interior. Then, the Flock Birds taking over a sizable expanse, scaring off predators, never social-distancing, usually a-chatter. And their leaders? That must be Adrienne Rich, among the many dark-eyed juncos on the ground, under the feeder—but which one?

———

It gets confusing. You could think yourself proudly and decidedly a Solitary Creeper making the rounds each morning on a thick-trunked old maple out back, looking for tasty insects, but in fact you're somewhere in the middle of a flock of yellow warblers over Ohio, on your way to Mexico for the winter. Who knew?

The poet Bill Knott (definitely a Solitary Creeper) allowed me to take his evening workshop at Columbia College in Chicago in 1974, for free. Working a crummy job post-college, I could honestly say, "I have no money," probably the only private conversation I ever had with Knott. He shrugged at my pathetic request, a gesture I understood as goodwill and maybe a yes—his "sure, why the hell not?" that followed making it clear. The first day of class, its initial few moments, he stared at the seated circle of us. He asked point blank who we were "imitating" in our poems.

"I don't imitate anyone!" we all, in our own ways, cried out, wounded by the question. At the end of everyone's short, impassioned soliloquy of denial, Knott shook his head: "Now I know one thing about you—you're all liars. So, let me ask that again, in another way. Who are you reading who you really, really, *really* like?"

We went around once more—*Charles Simic, Gwendolyn Brooks, Sylvia Plath, James Tate, Lucille Clifton*, and so on, though one shy throwback time-traveler whispered, *Gerard Manley Hopkins*. To that, the generous curmudgeon Bill Knott looked mildly amused, the rest of us simply perplexed.

Which brings up another point about poetry—there are fashions—and it is *always thus*. We're stuck, or at least start, in our own time and place; we're beholden, and usually keep going in its watery current for a while. Always, there is a house wine to go for first, it being the most available and already vetted, automatically palatable, familiar—not to mention, cheaper—a winning combo. To test this, read the entire work of anyone start to finish and follow the movement of tone, syntax, repeated imagery, the habits of dream and argument that echo but then for the most part eventually work *against* those writing in that same early era and wheelhouse.

Consider where Dickinson's sing-song came from, in spite of her saving-grace chronic weirdness. Years ago, I looked through the magazines she'd read, their relentless sheltering of truly bad poems—melodrama galore, predictable turns of thought and feeling, their doggerel groan, all default moves of the nineteenth century's flood of periodical verse. And Keats: a Ouija board chat with him would reveal how chronically he worried the ways those higher on the great (scathing) chain of poet-beings around him would measure his strange work, though of course he cherished Milton and Shakespeare to his last breath. It's good to time-travel for heroes; what the hell. There's more oxygen to spare.

The fact is it's always a mixtape. First books especially test the waters of what's hot right now, and more importantly, what isn't—what's to be avoided, scorned, if not erased, in the process. Though first books honor old habits, too, most of us, early or late, do censor ourselves, consciously or by autopilot, a kind of osmosis as we become our own "poetry police" via our quarrel with what we're convinced has ruined poems in the past, at times because others we trust think so. It's a way that poets enter *theory*. Consider Whitman, his call to bury the Brits, to champion American imagery and speech and sadness and yahoo a kind of instruction manual for the fresh democratic scope and sweep of his *Leaves of Grass*. Or Ezra Pound's frantic rant: his *make it new*. He'd no doubt agree with this assertion—"All the poetry published in America today is too old-fashioned." That's Robert Bly, some forty years after Pound, throwing down his gauntlet on page one of his outrageously amusing, combative, near-visionary journal called *The Fifties*, then *The Sixties*, finally *The Seventies*, wherein he regularly dismissed the verse currently in vogue as largely academic, dull, obvious, abstract, predigested, opting instead for a more surreal poetic vein, largely inspired by the poets he was translating: Pablo Neruda, Gunnar Ekelöf, César Vallejo, Georg Trakl.

It was a generational shift of tectonic plates, shattering traditional rhyme, meter, poetic shape for something wilder, weirder, and irresistible to so many. Famously, that would be Robert Lowell, Gwendolyn Brooks, James Wright, Adrienne Rich, Theodore Roethke, and others, experts nevertheless in the older and more formal methods of the art. They'd been there, done that. One can include Ginsberg here, and the forever-young Dr. Williams, a throwback doing doggerel at first who nevertheless eked out fresh habits in his own poems and inspired at least two generations to come (and maybe or maybe not thanked his college pal Pound for it). If we could track those transformations on a heart monitor, someone would be screaming for the nurse. Certainly a bit of serious screaming did go on, usually coming from long-established and cranky literary critics unnerved by change.

It's an old idea that's always new. Rebellion equals imaginative growth equals big trouble plus big rewards. Or not.

Closer to our time, Larry Levis comes to mind, lost to us tragically early at forty-nine. His coming-of-age poems reflect the mode of *their* time, the late 1960s and early '70s, which demanded short lines, a dose of the surreal, an ironic but earnest stance, and personal anecdote however altered out of nostalgia into an often-political *edgy*. (Backdrop: the Vietnam War, three game-changing political assassinations, heroic unrest via the Black Arts Movement and the brave work toward civil rights.) That fractured, passionate era invited enjambment for breathlessness and present tense for immediacy, went heavy on first person and a repetitive, declarative syntax. Now we might say all of this was *trending*. Because certainly you don't have to go all the way to Spain to run with the bulls. Anyone can wear the pale shirt and red kerchief required.

But curiosity and thus originality require years and nerve. You remember and you forget, both being crucial. Eventually, for Levis, it came down to a meditative line, a deepening feel for loss well past poetry's knee-jerk self-absorption. It meant a voice in love with pattern and repetition, dreamingly seductive, elegant and at a distance yet carefully intimate (is that the definition of "seductive"?), plus a cultural widening to poems that welcomed a genuine sense of history and the importance of the Latinx community to his native California, his easy-going wit muted to *poignant*, still surreal but the emphasis on *real*, images growing stranger but fully accurate, precise. The poems continued to explore the personal, to have a feel for the regional and the universal, to hold the impulse to assert but remain more narratively grounded, now, while retaining his old lyric flight. It could get bloody, too close for comfort.

Here are bits of the first section of "Elegy with an Angel at Its Gate"—from his last drafted collection, *Elegy*, published posthumously, the book's title taking up the poetic form that traditionally honors loss and how to think about loss. If Levis started out in the flock by taking up the poetic habits of the early 1970s only to move into his Solitary Creeper phase, this poem keeps both approaches but his *we* takes charge from the first—assuming Flock Bird status of a new sort, toward a vision that repeats its assertions through time, forward and back, to include all of us. Thus, this passage concerning how we disappear into something immense, joined to—

> . . . everyone, part of the horses bending
>
> Their necks to graze, part of every law,
> Part of each Apache heirloom for sale
> In a window, part of the wedding cake,
>
> Part of the smallpox epidemic, part of God . . .

But this breathless listing doesn't end, not yet. It goes on in its wily tercet way to gather up roads and weather or the "tenderest parting of flesh . . ." On to the "open doors of boxcars" and silk bedclothes, drive-in movies, a slaughterhouse with "its fly-covered windows," a young woman brushing her hair, how clean pillowcases and sheets fill the room with scent. Finally it is a vastly communal thing. Skip to how we all are "part of a vast revolution, of an age of revolutions—"

Then this, from another poem in *Elegy*—

> I do not wish to interfere, Reader, with your solitude—
> So different from my own . . .

Really? It strikes me that this Flock Bird turned solo flyer, then back to the great plural *we* of the flock, seems finally to carry a simple longing *to* interfere, and enter a kind of Duo, an "I/thou" status. It's in that aching direct address, its very targeted aim—*Reader*. And buried under it is a quieter, unspoken and archaic *oh Reader*, reaching even farther back.

So loneliness is rendered as shared solitude. In that sense, poetry's ache, however private, is universal, timeless, abrupt, political. Robert Frost is known for his cautionary "no surprise for the writer, no surprise for the reader" but less so for his companion advice—no *tears* for the writer, no *tears* for the reader—thus raising the stakes, be it one poem or a whole lifetime of poems.

Those tears—well, that's another trapdoor to open and follow down, not to sentimentality or nostalgia but to the grace and ferocity and nuance that Levis was after.

———

So much for poetry.

As for real birds, you can travel and take note. There are spots in the world filled with mountains, sky, a glimpse of blue water, and many large birds swoop and glide, and where one would think the red-tailed hawk with its splendid, scary gravitas would be a Solitary Creeper, a hunger machine just passing through. But it settles down—mates for life, tends to each day-by-day. This particular Duo often returns to the same nest year after year. What homebodies, these raptors, birds of prey that nevertheless—I've seen them—wait absolutely still, alone atop trees or on telephone lines, shrieking down to terrify tiny passerines like sparrows and wrens.

Which suggests more trouble, complicated and dark as a poem can be. Think of the startlingly tender (but is it tender?) loyalty of the vulture, another bird that partners up faithfully until its chosen other disappears forever, which could take a decade or more. Think how pointedly and causally it partakes of the dead on whatever near or distant road. Then there's the dove, with its soothing early morning litany, also mated for life, living up to its red-letter gig in our tiresome wedding day iconography.

But beware, I suppose, of *all* categories in the first place. After all, those sweet things can be vicious, doves with their wings back at an angle, ready to attack at the slightest irritation.

# POETICS: A STATEMENT

I was asked, but I'm not sure what a statement of poetics is.

1) A description of process from no to maybe to a full yes and *its* maybe?

2) An itinerary?

3) An aerial view?

4) A wish? A regret?

I regret that I don't believe that people really change—which is probably why I haven't written fiction, at least not yet. It's those stubborn bits in us, the unyielding eternal and hopeless bits, what seems to stay in the side vision, dark spots hanging on after the flash of the camera. But they don't always flash. They can purr, click, make a small muffled noise. And the photographer suddenly looks up at the world. But it's the dark spots that most matter to me.

Which is to say, images haunt. I understand that most of my poems are driven by images, though more and more I'm drawn by voice and what I do now seems a looser thing, a more meditative act. My work involves the daily odd things I see—the run-over, road-kill glove in the street, the sound of a child crying down through an elevator shaft when I stood last fall waiting three floors below, or the workmen outside my mother's hospital room not long before her death, how intent they were, fixing the roof. There's a small paring knife at the heart of these images, a complication, a stirring, a danger. I recognize such things as the beginning of poems. *Maybe* the beginning of poems. Which must mean I do believe in the *part* and the mysterious way it suggests the whole. But nothing is whole though wholenss is the human dream. Poems are never whole or, as was once famously said, never finished. I'm drawn to the truth in that. So this peculiar genre continues to fascinate. It's deeply humbling. No one on the planet really knows what a poem is or can be.

What's crucial is time and patience, though a poem can flash, can quickly fill itself in. Some very fine poets begin with a mission, with a sense of cultural and political expanse. I admire that a great deal. But to be honest—and this repeats itself to me, this thought that I often say out loud—it's mainly what I call my begging bowl theory: you empty out and work with what comes, careful to hold back intention, which has almost nothing to do with writing poems. An image. Maybe an idea. And there's a voice, of course. One goes quiet enough to follow these things where they might go. One is conscious and not conscious at all. It's a strange negotiation. Intimate. Often unnerving.

I hope, in fact, for unnerving. Then the revision. Imagine sitting with a friend who has lapsed into a coma. And you sit there and wait for any turn of muscle and nerve, a sign, a change in breathing that might realign everything. There's a lot of simple staring involved, trying to figure where the heat is in the poem, the weight, something that shifts or cuts at an angle, painful or not. *Discovery* is probably too large—I can't call it that exactly—though the words *self* and *world* are involved. But it can be small. Or it can, for a moment, seem huge.

# POETRY IN THE PLAGUE YEAR

A‍bove the desk where I write is a large pencil drawing of my son made by our artist daughter-in-law, given to me for Christmas some years back. Tucked into its frame is a color photograph of my grandson at age six, looking straight on and quite jauntily into the world, *as is* and to come. Also edged in there is a popular bumper sticker that never made it to the back end of my car: WHAT WOULD WALT WHITMAN DO?

Yes! What *would* he do now, that hack journalist turned major poet, that writer of what at the time was considered near-pornography in many quarters, his newly published *Leaves of Grass* passed around and savored in probably the (now) most famous law office in the history of Springfield, Illinois. And what of that one night recounted by biographer Daniel Mark Epstein? Abraham Lincoln himself took the book home for a longer read, only to save it at the last second from "being purified in fire" when Mary Todd Lincoln tried to put her literary criticism to good use, or so the future president apparently told compatriots at his law office the next day, when he returned the book intact. Some legends ring true.

I love to think of Lincoln reading Whitman. Maybe he heard traces of the Bible and Shakespeare that he'd taken to heart in his youth—pretty much the only books available on the frontier, where formal education was scanty. The long passages of each he committed to memory then must have been the fire and fuel behind the reserved and eloquent prose he found in himself those years later in Washington, where both men lived but apparently never met.

Lincoln reading Whitman! These days, it's a pleasure and rare relief to imagine someone in charge at the highest level during stricken times who would be attentive to cherished lines like—

> I believe a leaf of grass is no less than the journeywork of the stars,
> And the pismire is equally perfect, and a grain of sand, and the
>     egg of the wren,
> And the tree-toad is a chef-d'oeuvre for the highest,
> And the running blackberry would adorn the parlors of heaven,
> And the narrowest hinge in my hand puts to scorn all
>     machinery, . . .

All machines? Respirators and virus testers, too? Perhaps, more to Mrs. Lincoln's shocked and disapproving point in those long-ago, pre-social-distancing days:

> Blind loving wrestling touch! Sheathed hooded
>     sharptoothed touch!
> Did it make you ache so leaving me?

Poetry isn't therapy but it *can* open. Is there a case to be made for poetry in this plague year?

I don't care that much for argument. Instead, I'm amazed at how this first, most mysterious genre changes when the world does, how it deepens, is newly felt, induces that tell-tale *gulp!* into silence, the backdrop and end of all good poems. That's where we abruptly find ourselves: in a rich emptiness where we pause and absorb.

It could be at that famous crossroads in Robert Frost again, the spot where his "two roads diverged in a yellow wood." Or that "rainbow, rainbow, rainbow!" moment in the rented boat with Elizabeth Bishop, right before she raises a hand to that "battered and venerable / and homely" creature pulled out of the sea, its eyes "tarnished tinfoil," five old hooks in its mouth from previous assaults like "medals with their ribbons / frayed and wavering." Then, her quietly triumphant final line: "And I let the fish go."

Sometimes it is given to us to understand why great poems are iconic, why they *mean* beyond anyone's hope that they might mean. And thus, a possibility—a keyhole to the much larger.

# CELLULAR CHANGE

⌒

I have this acute flash, of the kitchen in Maine where we lived in the mid-1980s, 5 A.M., the woodstove's bright eye, my little lamp, and there had been a snow overnight. The enormous plow came doggedly roaring down the street, a muffled sound indoors but its eerie colored lights unmistakable, briefly pulsing the room. I was reading Robert Lowell, his poem "The Old Flame," which ends with that moment: "In one bed and apart, // we heard the plow / groaning up hill—/ a red light, then a blue, / as it tossed off the snow / to the side of the road." Oh my god, I thought. I'm *living* this poem! It leapt off the page.

Not a new thought, that life's real accretions allow a *re*entry into art. After all, disappointment opened up Larkin, as did growing older and crankier. One's own griefs, large and small, eventually turn idle appreciation for Bishop's "One Art" into a click, a *yes* so dark it can be unbearable to read again. I remember hearing a self-proclaimed nonreader of poetry on the radio once, a doctor, nevertheless holding forth on the piece, pretty much saying that. Knowing its backstory, who precisely Bishop meant by the *you* of "—Even losing you (the joking voice, a gesture / I love)" doesn't add much. (Lowell? Or Lota, her long-term partner who took her own life? No, it turns out to be a separation, short-term, from her final friend and lover.) But by then, reading the poem down to this serious closure, we have our own longer losses to think about, thank you. Bishop allows for that; in fact, she has invited it. Still, it must be that Bishop's earlier, graver sorrows press hard on the way she ends her poem.

I want Frost in here, saved in the nick of time from my total contempt by my having to memorize "After Apple-Picking" in graduate school, in a Modern Poetry class. I chose the piece, being fond of apples, of fall, and it fit the number of lines required in one efficient swoop. Yet, running it through my body for years now, reciting it again and again, has changed how I know this poem until *knowing* has become cellular-strange.

As one of Frost's greatest hits, the poem carries inside what routinely shines—or annoys—about this poet: his folksy "real" subjects, his vernacular speech, those moves based on what he called "sentence sounds," less keyed to line and its weight than we seem to be now. But his syntax turns and gives way; it hovers and floats. So, I realized, by maybe the eight-hundredth time I let the poem drop out loud through me, how lightly the piece bears its rich meaning (unlike Eliot, whom I also memorized, a bit from his forever ponderous, four-thousand-pound "Four Quartets"). Frost makes such a winding, spindly, supple thing of thinking itself.

Gradually—and this deepens for me, every time—his poem is so surprisingly surreal, especially in the transitions, that skimmed piece of ice, for instance, held up to melt, to blur the very real "hoary grass," thus launching the great hallucinatory drift which *is* this poem. If I close my eyes now to picture its shape, I see a kind of pointillist interior, a network of dizzying lines and dots of color coming to life—those truly weird "magnified apples" in and out, "stem end and blossom end."

As for life's accumulations, my years of house and yard husbandry (even as a child, put routinely to such work) tell me how accurately Frost renders the exhaustion of physical labor, not even sleep an escape from its temporary ravages as the poet *relives* what should be a sweet dream but isn't—the disturbing sway and bend of ladder and bough, that "rumbling sound / Of load on load of apples coming in." That the *real* is the crucial element in what grows *surreal*—what haunts, what stays, and certainly what Frost handles so gracefully here—seems suddenly obvious.

But his other odd triumphs still puzzle me, and will for a long time. Like how he does an impossible thing, his so perfectly natural and *not* comic move at the end as he considers asking a woodchuck—a woodchuck, for god's sake—about the much darker nature of "whatever sleep it is," the one we're all in for.

I admit: I've liked this poem well enough from the start. Now I'm in so deep, I'm past love. It's not an about-face but a slow *coming to* gotten from the body itself, from running Frost's wily sentences through my nerves and muscles and breath, three decades now. It's not exactly the power of poems to change because we change, or how certain pieces define for us, finally and mysteriously, what we call poetry. I really don't know what it is.

# ACKNOWLEDGMENTS

Warm thanks to the editors of the following publications who welcomed these pieces (some since slightly revised or with new titles) to their pages or website.

And to the students and faculty of the MFA Program for Writers at Warren Wilson College, who might recall a few of these wee essays from the lectures I gave there, and who, in turn, offered me valuable comments.

I also want to thank poets Jen Webb and Paul Hetherington at the University of Canberra's International Poetry Studies Institute, host of my 2019 Fulbright; poet and novelist Paul Collis, who teaches Indigenous studies and creative writing at Canberra; and other Australian poets—Lizz Murphy, Judith Crispin, Sarah St. Vincent Welch, Hazel Hall, Geoff Page, and Kevin Brophy—who opened that extraordinary world to me. Certainly I'm delighted that one of my oldest friends, artist and poet Berkeley Brown McChesney, painted the stunning cover art for this book. And I truly appreciate the good work of Northwestern University Press editors, especially Anne Gendler and Marisa Siegel.

My loving gratitude to David Dunlap, first reader always.

*American Poetry Review*:
"The Trouble Gene"
"Spellcheck"
"In the Middle of Even This: Poetry"

"Oh No"
"Wild Blue Yonder"

*AWP Chronicle*:
"In the Dreamtime"

*A Broken Thing: Poets on the Line*, edited by Emily Rosko and Anton
Vander Zee (University of Iowa Press, 2011):
"Secret Life"

*Copper Nickel*:
"Instead Instead"

*Field*:
"Saint Kevin, Saint Blackbird"
"Some Moments in 'Moment Fugue' "
"Bent as I Was, Intently"

*Georgia Review*:
Pilgrimage
The Great Silence

*The Dangerous Women Project* (online publication of the Institute for
Applied Study in the Humanities at the University of Edinburgh):
"The Other Wordsworth"

*Narrative*:
"Oh"
"Shirt"
"Computer Blurs, Black-Outs, Audio Hiccups, and Stardust"
"Poetry in the Plague Year"

*New England Review*:
"Embarrassment"
"Audio"

*The New Ohio Review*:
   "Everything All at Once"
   "Cellular Change"

*Poet of the Month* (May 2006), online site curated by Mark Jarman, 1997–2007:
   "A Statement of Poetics"

*Poetry*:
   "Ah"
   "Melodrama"

*Poetry's Harriet* online blog:
   "The Burning"
   "Adverbs or Not"

*The Poetry Review* (UK):
   "Ah," reprinted via an exchange with *Poetry*

*Poetry Daily*:
   "Unlimited"

*The Rag-Picker's Guide to Poetry: Poems, Poets, Process*, edited by Eleanor Wilner and Maurice Manning (Ann Arbor: University of Michigan Press, 2013):
   "How to Dissect a Cadaver"

*The Yale Review*:
   "Boredom"

*Third Coast*:
   "Middle Kingdom" (The first version of this essay was a talk, "Midwest Writers and the Middle Kingdom," given at the Gathering of Writers at the Indiana Writers Center in Indianapolis, on March 26, 2016; Executive Director Barbara Shoup.)

# WORKS CONSULTED

Auden, W. H. *The Collected Shorter Poems*. New York: Random House, 1985.

Berryman, John. *77 Dream Songs*. Farrar, Straus & Giroux, 1964.

———. National Book Award for Poetry acceptance speech, 1969.

Bishop, Elizabeth. *The Complete Poems, 1927–1979*. New York: Farrar, Straus & Giroux, 1983.

Borges, Jorge Luis. *Labyrinths*. New York: New Directions, 1962.

Boruch, Marianne. *Cadaver, Speak*. Port Townsend, WA: Copper Canyon Press, 2016.

———. *Dark Bestiary*. Port Townsend, WA: Copper Canyon Press, 2021.

Breugel, Pieter (the Elder). *Landscape with the Fall of Icarus*, c. 1560. Oil on canvas, 73.5 × 112 cm. Royal Museums of Fine Arts of Belgium.

Brown, Ashley. "An Interview with Elizabeth Bishop." *Shenandoah* 17 (Winter 1966), 3–19.

Bunyan, John, *The Pilgrim's Progress*. Oxford: Oxford University Press, 2003.

Burroway, Janet. *Writing Fiction: A Guide to Narrative Craft*. Boston: Little, Brown, 1982.

Campbell, Rev. Paul E., and Sister Mary Donatus MacNickle. *Voyages in English*, 8th ed. Chicago: Loyola University Press, 1951.

Carroll, Paul, ed. *The Young American Poets*. Chicago: Big Table, 1969.

Carson, Ciaran. *Belfast Confetti*. Winston-Salem, NC: Wake Forest University Press, 1989.

————. *The New Estate*. Loughcrew Oldcastle, Ireland: Gallery Press, 1988.

Clare, John. *Selected Poems*. New York: Penguin, 2000.

Clifton, Lucille. *Mercy*. Rochester, NY: BOA Editions, 2004.

Conrad, Joseph. *Victory*. New York: Penguin, 2016.

Crane, Hart. *Hart Crane: Complete Poems and Selected Letters*, edited by Langdon Hammer. New York: Library of America, 2006.

Dickinson, Emily. *The Complete Poems of Emily Dickinson*, edited by Thomas H. Johnson. Boston: Little, Brown, 1960.

————. *Letters of Emily Dickinson*, edited by Thomas H. Johnson. Cambridge, MA: Harvard University Press, 1997.

Dunlap, Will. "The Salvation of Doctor MacLeod" (unpublished novel).

Edson, Russell. *The Intuitive Journey and Other Works*. New York: Harper and Co., 1973.

Eliot, T. S. *The Complete Poems and Plays, 1909–1950*. New York: Harcourt, Brace & World, 1952.

Epstein, Daniel Mark. *Lincoln and Whitman: Parallel Lives in Civil War Washington*. New York: Ballantine, 2004.

Finlay, Victoria. *Color: A Natural History of the Palette*. New York: Random House, 2002.

Frost, Robert. *The Poetry of Robert Frost*, edited by Edward Connery Lathem. New York: Holt, Rinehart and Winston, 1969.

————. *The Selected Prose of Robert Frost*, edited by Hyde Cox and Edward Connery Lathem. New York: Holt, Rinehart and Winston, 1966.

Gass, William. *Fiction and the Figures of Life*. New York: Vintage, 1972.

Glück, Louise. *The Triumph of Achilles*. New York: Ecco, 1985.

Hass, Robert. *Twentieth Century Pleasures: Prose on Poetry*. New York: Ecco, 1984.

Heaney, Seamus. *Selected Poems, 1966–1996*. New York: Farrar, Straus & Giroux, 1998.

————. *Crediting Poetry*. New York: Farrar, Straus and Giroux, 2014.

Hoagland, Tony. *Real Sofistikashun*. Minneapolis: Graywolf Press, 2006.

Hopkins, Gerard Manley. *The Prose and Poems of Gerard Manley Hopkins*. New York: Penguin, 1986.

Hughes, Langston. *The Collected Poems of Langston Hughes*. New York: Knopf, 1994.

Jensen, Laura. "Dialogues with Northwest Writers" (Greg Simon interviews Laura Jensen). *Northwest Review* 20, nos. 2 & 3 (1982): 79–93.

————. *Memory*. Port Townsend, WA: Dragon Gate, 1982.

————. *Shelter*. Port Townsend, WA: Dragon Gate, 1985.

Keats, John. *Complete Poems and Selected Prose of John Keats*, edited by Harold Briggs. New York: Random House, 1951.

————. *The Letters of John Keats*, edited by Maurice Buxton Forman. Oxford: Oxford University Press, 1931.

Kelly, Brigit Pegeen. *The Orchard*. Rochester, NY: BOA Editions, 2004.

————. *Song*. Rochester, NY: BOA Editions, 1995.

Larkin, Philip. *Collected Poems*. London: Noonday, 1989.

Levis, Larry. *Elegy.* Pittsburgh, PA: University of Pittsburgh Press, 1997.

MacLeish, Archibald. *Collected Poems, 1872–1982.* New York: Houghton, Mifflin, Harcourt, 1985.

McDermott, H. J. *The Trappist Monk: A Concise History of the Order of Reformed Cistercian, with a Sketch of the Abbey of New Melleray.* Whitefish, MT: Kessinger Publishing, 2007.

Menotti, Gian Carlo. *The Consul.* Conducted by Nino Sanzogno at La Scala in Milan, 1954. Naxos Historical. Released June 2010, 2 compact discs.

Merton, Thomas. *When the Trees Say Nothing: Writings on Nature,* edited by Kathleen Deignan. Notre Dame, IN: Sorin Books, 2003.

Moore, Marianne. *The Complete Poems.* New York: Macmillan, 1981.

Oppen, George. "Selections from George Oppen's *Daybook.*" *Iowa Review* 18, no. 3 (1988): 1–17.

Orr, Peter. "An Interview with Sylvia Plath." British Broadcasting Corporation, October 30, 1962.

Sexton, Anne. *The Complete Poems.* New York: Houghton Mifflin, 1981.

Simic, Charles. *Selected Poems, 1963–1983.* New York: George Braziller, 1990.

Perillo, Lucia. *On the Spectrum of Possible Deaths.* Port Townsend, WA: Copper Canyon Press, 2012.

Plath, Sylvia. *Ariel: The Restored Edition: A Facsimile of Plath's Manuscript, Reinstating Her Original Selection and Arrangement.* New York: Harper Collins, 2004.

———. *The Collected Poems.* New York: Harper, 1981.

———. Drafts of "Poppies in October." The Ariel Collection of the Manuscript Collection of Sylvia Plath, William Allan Neilson Library, Smith College, Northampton, MA.

Pliny the Elder. *Natural History*. Cambridge, MA: Harvard University Press, 1935.

Pound, Ezra. "A Few Don'ts by an Imagiste." *Poetry: A Magazine of Verse* 1, no. 6 (March 1913): 200–208.

———. *Literary Essays*. New York: New Directions, 1935.

———. *Make It New: Essays by Ezra Pound*. London: Faber and Faber, 1935; New Haven, CT: Yale University Press, 1935.

Prado, Adelia. *The Alphabet in the Park: Selected Poems of Adelia Prado*, translated by Ellen Dore Watson. Middletown, CT: Wesleyan University Press, 1990.

Prejean C.S.J., Sister Helen. *Dead Man Walking*. New York: Penguin, 1994.

Puccini, Giacomo. *La Boheme*. Conducted by Herbert von Karajan. Berlin Philharmonic, 1987. Decca 421 0492, 2 compact discs.

Reed, A. W. *Aboriginal Myths: Tales of the Dreamtime*. Sydney, Australia: New Holland Publishers, 2002.

Roethke, Theodore. *The Collected Poems*. New York: Doubleday, 1975.

———. *Letters of Theodore Roethke*, edited by Ralph Mills Jr. Seattle: University of Washington Press, 1968.

Sandburg, Carl. *Chicago Poems*. New York: Henry Holt, 1916.

Stevens, Wallace. *The Collected Poems of Wallace Stevens*. New York: Random House, 1982.

———. *Opus Posthumous*. New York: Knopf, 1957.

Szymborska, Wisława. "The Poet in the World." Nobel Lecture, 1966. www.nobelprize.org/prizes/literature/1996/Szymborska/lecture.

———. *View with a Grain of Sand: Selected Poems*. New York: Harcourt Brace, 1993.

Tate, James. Introduction to *The Best American Poetry, 1997*. New York: Scribner, 1997.

Three Stooges (Moe Howard, Larry Fine, and Curly Howard) in the "Niagara Falls" routine. *Gents Without Cents,* a short subject by Columbia Pictures, dir. Jules White, released September 22, 1944. Running time 19.02 minutes.

Tonks, Rosemary. *Bedouin of the London Evening: Collected Poems & Selected Prose.* Hexham, UK: Bloodaxe Books, 2014.

Twain, Mark (Samuel Langhorne Clemens). *Adventures of Huckleberry Finn.* New York: Norton, 1998.

Verdi, Giuseppe. *Aida.* Conducted by Georg Solti. Orchestra Del Teatro Dell' Opera Di Roma, 1961. Decca 417 416-1, 3 compact discs.

Voigt, Ellen Bryant. *The Flexible Lyric.* Athens, GA: University of Georgia Press, 1999.

———. *Kyrie.* New York: W. W. Norton, 1995.

———. *The Lotus Flowers.* New York: W. W. Norton, 1988.

———. *Two Trees.* New York: W. W. Norton. 1992.

Ward, Aileen. *John Keats: The Making of a Poet.* New York: Farrar, Straus and Giroux, 1986.

Watts, May Theilgaard. *Reading the Landscape: An Adventure in Ecology.* New York: Macmillan, 1957.

Wehr, Wesley. "Elizabeth Bishop: Conversations and Class Notes." *Antioch Review* 39, no. 3 (1981): 319–28.

Werner, Marta L. *Emily Dickinson's Open Folios: Scenes of Reading, Surfaces of Writing.* Ann Arbor: University of Michigan Press, 1996.

Whitman, Walt. *Leaves of Grass.* New York: Dutton, 1971.

Wordsworth, Dorothy. *The Grasmere and Alfoxden Journals,* edited by Pamela Woolf. Oxford: Oxford University Press, 2002.

Wright, Wilbur and Orville. *The Published Writings of Wilbur and Orville Wright,* edited by Peter Jakab and Rick Young. Washington, DC: Smithsonian Institution Press, 2000.

Zweig, Paul. *Walt Whitman: The Making of a Poet.* New York: Basic Books, 1984.

# INDEX OF NAMES